To
for look...
Native gifts upon your
Spirit Path — Peace & Joy
Rainbow Eagle

The Universal

Peace Shield

of Truths:
Ancient American Indian
Peace Shield Teachings

Rainbow Eagle: Seventh Fire Peace Shield Teacher

RAINBOW LIGHT & COMPANY
ANGEL FIRE, NEW MEXICO

In remembrance
Of
Debbie Blankenship

Published by
Rainbow Light & Company
P.O. Box 1434
Angel Fire, NM 87710
Copyright © 1996
by Rolland J. Williston

First Printing - October 1996
Second Printing - April 1997

ISBN 0-9655217-0-2

Printed on recycled paper
RECYCLED PAPER

Illustration Artist: Tannoth Badger Franklin
Author Photo: Sapokni Onna
Manuscript Editing: Dr. Margo Baldwin, Becky Lachance,
                     Mosses Moon Eagle
Typist: Sky Jiménez
Co-Editor: Annette "Snow Eagle" Keenan

For information on workshops, seminars, speaking engagements and teaching groups
contact:

Keenan and Associates, Inc.
P.O. Box 171
West Liberty, OH 43357 (937)465-2249

Rainbow Eagle's Web Site: http://www.irnoise.com/rainboweagle

CONTENTS

1978 Religious Freedom Act of Congress - Seven Fire Prophecies of the Ojibwa/Anishinabe Nation - The placing of the Peace Shield with Rainbow Eagle - Hidden sacred records to come forth in the Seventh Fire - 500 Year Prophecy of the Condor and the Eagle to fly together - Hopi Prophecy, Pahana and the Stone Tablets - The role of visionaries and prophecy to community - Earth people are at the "Y"/crossroads - Purpose of the Peace Shield to Earthwalkers.

Asked by the Elders and "Gram"/Seneca Grandmother Twylah Nitsch to write a book - Teach those who don't know, reach as many as you can - Spirit said, " . . . begin your next work" - Change loses its sting when . . . - The Sacred Shields and the Peace Chiefs.

VISITS WITH THE PEACE SHIELD TEACHER

"I am coming" - Beginning the wintery journey - Reminiscing of other visits with Native Elders - One did not argue over one's beliefs - The Peace Chief's visit to nearby Chippewa Reservation - Recovery of Indianness - My first Sacred Sweat Lodge Ceremony - Grandpa Frank Foolscrow and the Sacred Pipe - Native community council meeting and gift by Elder - Irv's steadfast position as Peace Chief - Tribute to female leadership/spirituality - AA program and the use of the Peace Shield and Sweat Lodge - With the Peace Shield Teacher - For me to teach this - A tribute to Irv Romans: Peace Chief - To present life beyond present understanding.

EARTH BOY AND THE SACRED COUNCIL: A STORY

An Anishinabe story of a boy who visits the Seven Sacred People and returns

with the Seven Gifts to his people - Gift of the Vision Quest and Sweat Lodge
- Preparing for first look at the Peace Shield.

PEACE SHIELD TEACHINGS: SOURCES OF SPIRITUAL
TEACHINGS/LAWS
> The Elder/Child relationship - Oral tradition - Symbolism and interpretation -
> Indian religion went underground - What does the Red Road mean -
> Teachings of the Eagle Feathers - Repression of Native religion - Why is there
> more interest in Native things now - Must carefully choose teachers of the Red
> Road - Ceremony and responsibility - Teaching of the Two.

PEACE SHIELD TEACHINGS: THE GREAT SPIRITUAL LODGE OF
THE CREATOR
> The outer blue circle and the very center of the Peace Shield - Wolf and the
> Original Man - Truths "To Become the Flowering Tree" - Concepts of good
> and bad - "It's a good day to die" - Sacred Number Seven - Zero Chiefs
> teachings - Teachings of the Number Four - Four levels of spirituality - The
> Vision of Gitchie Manitou - The Four Creations - An introduction to Big
> Foot/Wildman - Animal symbolism: buffalo, coyote, wolf, Inktomi the spider -
> Respect one's personal vision - Get ready for doors yet to be opened.

PEACE SHIELD TEACHINGS: REFLECTIONS OF THE CREATOR
> The second circle around the Creator - Twelve Gatekeepers - Considering the
> challenge to be respectful of all religions - Native reflections of the Creator -
> U.S. Constitution and the Great Iroquois Confederacy - Lesson of awareness -
> The Morning Star Visitor - Quetzalcoatl - Deganawidah and Hiawatha -
> Twelve Lodge Poles - Seven Drum Religion - Other reflections of the Creator
> - In harmony with elements for ceremony - Some historical perspectives - My
> challenge to Native People - Some parallels between Red Road spirituality
> and Christianity.

TEACHINGS/TRUTHS AROUND THE PEACE SHIELD
> Gifts and limitations discussed - <u>Looking to the East</u>: The Eagle and the
> Seven Seats - Teachings of the Eagle - Seven Clan system - Lessons of Sacred
> Tobacco - A Prayer to the East - <u>Looking to the South</u>: Rabbit and the
> Prophecy of the Seven Fires - Teachings of the Rabbit - Seven Fire Prophecy -
> Lessons of Cedar - A Prayer to the South - <u>Looking to the West</u>: The Bear and

the Seven Megis Shells/Spiritual Journeys - Brooke Medicine Eagle:
Women's Moon Time - Teaching of Sage - A Prayer to the West - <u>Looking to
the North</u>: Deer and the Seven Feather Gifts - Teachings of Sweetgrass - A
Prayer and Thank you to the Spirit Keepers of the North - Advice to those who
would honor these teachings of the Peace Shield.

A STEP INTO THE FUTURE - JOURNEY TOWARDS THE LIGHT/SPIRITUAL LODGE OF THE CREATOR

A Commentary

AMERICAN INDIAN STORIES TO BE TOLD WITH THE PEACE SHIELD

One:	The Great Mystery's Vision
Two:	Nokomis/Grandmother: A Creation Story
Three:	Rainbow Eagle: My Vision
Four:	NAPI Gets Angry
Five:	The Story of When the Snake Had Legs
Six:	Raven's Story
Seven:	Legend of the Cheyennes and Pawnees
Eight:	The Coming of the Salmon People
Nine:	The Story of Foolish Rabbit
Ten:	The Wolf's Vision Quest
Eleven:	Clay Pot Boy
Twelve:	Must Gather to Continue Life
Thirteen:	The Path Without End
Fourteen:	The Sacred Spring and Gifts of Corn and Meat
Fifteen:	The Last Rose
Sixteen:	The Pipe and the Eagle

ACKNOWLEDGEMENTS AND DEDICATIONS

This book is dedicated to those children of the present, called the Seventh Fire, including my children: Melina Kay, Rolland Jay, Rhonda and James Henry. To my father, Henry Silas Williston and mother, Mable - my love and gratitude.

It is for the children of the future generations that we preserve these Peace Shield Teachings. To Grandpa Frank Foolscrow, GF Wilsie Bitsie, Grandmothers Little Pigeon and Twylah Nitsch, Chief Leonard Dokis, Grandfather Hollis Little Creek, Gerald Melting Tallow, and many, many others who have taught me Native ways.

My thank you to Sun Dance Chief Jimmy Dubray, Harvy and Agnes Ross, Hawk Little John, Grandmother Louise Logan and Leland Logan who have invited me into their homes and teaching places. To Chuck and Dorothy Ross, Buck and Vickie Ghosthorse, Jack Sands, Ben Craft, Price Cockran, and many other Native brothers and sisters who encouraged my walk with Red Road spirituality. My gratitude to Wilber Hayden and Chuck Maples, who choose to live near reservations and often love Native people unconditionally. Thank you for your prayers - - Sun Dance Elders and community.

I give my appreciation for my companion, Sapokni Onna, as this book would not have been possible without her love, companionship, encouragement, and unconditional love of all life, everywhere.

Letter to the Reader

Hope Found in Teachings of an Ancient American Indian
Peace Shield
Revealed by Rainbow Eagle, Seventh Fire Peace Shield Teacher

I am a native person of Okla-Choctaw heritage, who has been entrusted and honored in this Seventh Fire to offer the teachings of an ancient Anishinabe (Ojibwa) Peace Shield of truth and instructions to the Human Family one last time. The ancient truths of this shield are older than many sources, including the Dead Sea Scrolls. Gathering and increasing truth's power to restore and amplify peace upon Mother Earth is the ultimate purpose of the Peace Shield.

A bundle was opened in early 1996 in a special ceremony to begin the sacred mission of the Peace Shield. Contained within the bundle is a sacred prayer pipe and large elk hide upon which the Peace Shield is drawn. "The Seven Fire Prophecy" foretold of this time to the ancient people. Seven prophets spoke of a Fire or Spiritual chapter which described things which would happen to the people. The Seventh Prophet said that native ways would be honored and the elders would again speak. Also shared was, the light skinned race would be given a choice between two roads: Destruction or the lighting of the Eighth and final fire, an age of peace, love, joy and oneness.

In addition, the Seventh Fire foretold of the signals which would be given to Native People so they would know when to act for the good of "All Relations". The signals would include environmental concerns, risks to the destruction of humanity, high levels of technology, Earth Changes, and finally freedom for Native

v

people to participate in their beliefs.

The Peace Shield is a reminder to Native people that in the Seventh Fire it would be their responsibility to assist and help bring the Human Family back together again. "These original truths of the Peace Shield are to be given to the Human Race for the last time so that each person can have what they need to decide the future of our Mother Earth." The Peace Shield teaches the value, beauty, wisdom and wonder of walking into the future with great faith and absolutely no fear. In the past, the Peace Shield provided community and personal stability; it now charters for human kind a journey into the blessed future.

The Peace Shield brings this challenge to all Earth Walkers - become more aware of and develop respect for all religions and ways of reaching toward the Creator. The Peace Shield has a specific circle that honors and holds the energy of those prophets, messengers and spiritual leaders who are the reflections or rays of light that emit the truths and glow of the Great Source/Creator. Unique to the Peace Shield is the bringing of a "sharing table" into the Lodge of the Creator. At this table, the Human Family can become aware of our neighbors that share this earthly planet. As each person, group and community of believers talks with each other, the outcome promised in many prophecies comes nearer.

I believe that spirituality lives **first** in one's personal expression of truth, **second**, in the choice to find companionship with others, and **third,** in the courage and self discipline to walk one's talk in the next "fire" or dimension of existence. One reminder is presented here for all to consider. Sacred scrolls and documents will be brought out of their concealment when the people return to spiritual ways "By Faith Alone." We must take time to reflect upon our native warriors and aborigines who exhibited no fear in purer cultural times.

A significant blessing, and gift, of the Peace Shield is its energy to balance oneself and groups. The task of spiritual beings in the Seventh Fire is the balancing or the strengthening of two aspects of our personal outlook on life. Having achieved this balancing of two truths, there develops within our spiritual being a totally new aspect within us. This new aspect, a third dimension of self, can assist and literally propel us into or toward a new reality of life, or step into the future.

Many of us are standing at some sort of "Y" in the road. I believe the Peace Shield within us and the Peace Shield(s) by ancient ones can shed light upon our journey back to the side of the Creator and Community. The future will be created by each one of us. Let us all anticipate and prepare, even celebrate our journey toward new realities of life.

To all my relations and the Universe,

Rainbow Eagle

The Universal Peace Shield of Truths

INTRODUCTION

In 1978, Native peoples, including those of Alaska and the Hawaiian Islands, were given religious freedom by an Act of Congress. Thus began the move of Earth People from the Sixth to the Seventh and final fire. As will be further explained, each "fire" represents a chapter of a spiritual age in which certain events were prophesied many thousands of years ago. This prophecy is called the "Seven Fire Prophecy" of the Anishinabe Nation (the ancient name for the Ojibwa/Chippewa Nation of the Great Lakes region of the United States). In this time of the Seventh Fire, these original truths, the teachings of the Peace Shields, are to be brought out for the last time. They are to be shared with all four races to help bring the human family back together again. The human race is truly standing before pathways toward either continued disharmony with nature or blessedness with universal oneness.

In the early 1980's, the last Peace Shield Teacher of the Anishinabe Nation called me to his home for two winter visits. He shared the teachings of the Peace Shield, an Ancient Anishinabe Drawing, with me and one other Native person before he "changed worlds" in 1984. Now there are only two to teach the Shield and put it into active use. Two additional apprentices help me make the teachings more available.

As a traditional person, I have placed a Sacred Prayer Pipe with the Peace Shield Bundle to be used whenever the Shield is opened and honored. I have often gone to the Peace Shield Prayer Pipe with much prayer and fasting to ask for guidance to convey these teachings in a good way. These revelations will be done with respect.

The Peace Shield can only be taught when there is no war, and now is the time for this old drawing to be revealed to the Earth Family. There are four door openings in this ancient Peace Shield for all the known truths of the world to enter into the Great Lodge of the Creator. The interpretation of the symbols and the spirit of community in the Peace Shield, also the gathering of truths from all sources, are fulfillment of ancient prophecy. These teachings are now being offered to spiritually-minded persons as a challenge to become joyful walkers into a wonderful and eventful future.

The Peace Shield wisdom is to be added to the wisdom of other sacred scrolls and records, such as the Dead Sea Scrolls, that have been and continue to be discovered. The purpose of these discoveries is to provide humanity with access to ancient and present knowledge. This knowledge will guide human choices and entry into the last fire, or spiritual chapter. Humanity must actively participate in the trail blazing of spiritual paths now. If there isn't great light at the end of our tunnels, then we must have all truths available to us now to build our faith in the Creator - the Great Mystery. There should be great optimism in the days in which we live.

In the Anishinabe teachings, the Sixth Fire (before the 1970's) was a time when all medicine people gathered the sacred bundles and scrolls that recorded the ceremonies. They placed these sacred bundles and scrolls in a hollowed-out log from the ironwood tree. It was then lowered over a cliff and buried where no one could find it. It is said that when the time came for Indian people to practice their religion without fear, a little boy would dream of where the ironwood log was buried. He would lead his people to that place.

It is said that the Ojibwa Nation kept their records on birch bark scrolls. These scrolls will be brought out of their concealment when the people return to spiritual ways "by faith alone." If they were to be brought out before then, the people would return to the Spirit Path out of fear, not out of faith, love and kindness. It is believed that the last time the scrolls were brought up to date was in 1915. For many years, people have searched for the scrolls. "Even when they are found, we will not have the ability to read them. This ability belongs to the few who were charged with keeping the scrolls."

Many indigenous Native people of "Turtle Island" (North America), as well as of Central and South America, are starting to take flight together. This is just as was stated in Incan prophecy that ". . . after 500 years of oppression, the eagle and the condor will fly together." I spoke with Willaru Huayta, spiritual messenger from South America, during one of his visits to Ohio. Steven McFadden described Willaru and his teachings in his book, *Profiles In Wisdom.*

Willaru Huayta emphasizes that he is not a shaman, nor is he a priest, or even a teacher. He is a "chasqui", a spiritual messenger in the tradition of the Inca. Specifically, he says he is a messenger of the Sun, and the message of solar wisdom that he bears is a synthesis of wisdom from all the traditions of the world. "I am a child of the universe," Willaru explains, "and my mission is planetary, even though the specific lore I know is from the Incan and Gnostic traditions."

"We have been waiting five hundred years," he says. "The Incan prophecies say that now, in this age, when the eagle of the North and the condor of the South fly together, the Earth will awaken. The eagles of the North cannot be free without the condors of the South. Now it is happening. Now is the time. The Aquarian Age is an era of light, an age of awakening, an age of returning to natural ways. Our generation is here to help begin this age, to prepare, through different schools, to understand the message of the heart, intuition and nature."

"Native people speak with the Earth. When consciousness awakens, we can fly high like the eagle or like the condor in 'El Condor Pasa'. Ultimately, you know, we are all native, because the word native comes from nature and we are all part of Mother Nature. She is inside us and we are inside her. We depend totally on the Earth, the Sun and the water."

I have been with, and witnessed, some of our present Elders, the Grandmothers and Grandfathers taking steps "off the reservation" to teach. Their willingness to share ancient truth is motivated by their nearness to the Divine Source - the Creator. Yet, they have received pointed criticism from their own people for sharing teachings of their traditions. Others, such as Lakota author Ed McGaa, write that it is time that spirituality be shared. In his book, *Mother Earth Spirituality*, McGaa writes:

"I believe, like Foolscrow, Eagle Feather, Sun Bear, Midnight Song, Rolling Thunder and a host of other traditional peoples, that it is time that spirituality is shared."

Many are aware of the sharing of the last 20-30 years by our Hopi Elders, Mayan brothers, Aborigines and others. They are innately connected to Mother Earth and to where we are in the cycling of Earth history. They are the "windows" to sacred records and instruments which surfaced in their times. Also shared has been prophecy stating that the Great Purifier/True White Brother, who some refer to as Pahana, the elder White Brother, would return bringing stone tablets to be placed together with hidden Hopi tablets. These tablets together form the Life Plan for those following the Great Spirit. Dan Katchongua, Hopi Elder, says, "This calls for all Indian Nations to become a brother under the one Great Spirit, to find the one central Life Plan and follow it and walk forward to the Good Life. Then we will help each other . . . we will uplift and support each other in our faith. For the white people (to) realize we must work together, then if they are faithful, they will help us to follow the Life Plan." Lomouaya, another Elder, relates, "By what sign to know of the coming of the Elder Brother . . . I will give you a sign by having certain stars fall, and when you see this sign, you will want to prepare to start to get rid of things that are burdening you so . . . you will have your burden in a light manner."

I believe that a spirit of "opening to more vision" is growing among all ages of human kind. The ancients, the Elders, are now finding spiritual residence within younger age groups. Younger "Elders" are taking their spiritual positions. Lakota leader, Orvil Lookinghorse, is keeper of the White Buffalo Calf Pipe and took part in the "coming out of the Ceremonial Pipe" of which I am caretaker. He remarked to me, "You are the youngest Pipe Carrier/Elder that I have met."

Some Native traditions speak of their prophecies as coming to an end. There is no end. Ancient calendars are not ending, but, I believe, merely recycling and signaling us of some bright and beautiful existence ahead. We are only reaching a point where there is a nearness to the cycle "starting all over again" - the re-emergence of divine participation in the path of human life and spiritual evolution. As a result, creativity and political freedoms are reaching high levels in many parts of the world.

Visionaries are to prepare the people for the present journey. They are to touch especially the minds and hearts of the young and to inform them to walk into the days ahead with pride and dignity. Their visions, wisdom and prophecies must become "hand-holds" and "signposts" along the path. These tools of vision will be used to create eternal optimism and assurance that the Creator/Great Mystery loves them and waits to enlighten their journey. Just as importantly, enlightened visionaries can cause many to open their eyes to realities yet to come. They establish a readiness and awareness of other life-forms from other places than on the surface of Mother Earth.

Because of the cyclical nature of life, each one of us

is able to experience visions at some level. By becoming more knowledgeable of natural laws and attuning our spirituality to reflect more of the Great Mystery within us, I am convinced that we can see into the future with spiritual eyes. We can see where we are going by utilizing the sacredness within us, the prophecies and teachings, such as the Medicine Wheel and the Peace Shield.

How do prophecies and ancient visions help humankind? First, prophecy identifies for our community, especially the young, where we are in relation to events of the past. Prophecy provides a sense of what to expect in the future and thus provides a "point of reference" for the community. The spiritual advisors and Elders, when asked, provide the connection between these prophecies and the natural law of the universe.

Second, prophecy gives meaning to what has already taken place. Some of our Native people today would benefit much from prophecy. Those who are very restless and unsettled, who expend aimless energy, would find balance in understanding of prophecy and having respect for our Elders. Having respect for our Elders is to understand their loyalty to, and journey through, past prophecy. We must more fully celebrate and honor all of the Elder's journeys, including the past prophecies of the Trail of Tears, Wounded Knee and other losses in Native history.

The dance of life, traditions and customs are, without doubt, returning. Another Anishinabe Elder, Hollis Little Creek, helped me to understand this principle more clearly when he said, "Nothing is lost. If it is needed again, the Great Spirit will bring it back to us." The ancients are present with us now, and their prayers are still being spoken. This gives us all more reason to walk with pride and in beauty knowing that the future is bright before us.

The third usefulness of prophecy is that it allows Native people to envision what lies ahead of us. The ideas of survival and vision of where we are going from this reality to the next reality are, I believe, unique to indigenous people. To Native people, there is no such thing as death. It is an anticipated journey toward the next world of reality. Death is only the "changing of worlds." The life of the Native person could be lived to the fullest because eternity was so firmly a part of Native Spirituality. Every moment was meaningful, every step a prayer, every event was to be experienced in as complete a way as possible. Consequently, Native people were free to be very intense storytellers, wisdom-keepers, craftspeople, fighters in battle and living of life close to natural laws. This living-in-the-moment placed value upon life and taught that life was to be given full attention - even in dream time. Each day was another gift from the Great Provider, given so we could learn more lessons. Our lessons were about how to walk in our relatedness to creation, in oneness with the Great Mystery and in harmony with the whole universe.

The Peace Shield tells of the Earth People being at a crossroad of life. We are at a "Y" in the road where we must choose what kind of future we want for ourselves and for future generations. We must choose either to seek the nearness of the Creator and a respectful relationship to each religion or grouping of truth, or continue a journey of separation from the eternity of all life which brings only more hard life-lessons. There is clear reason to be optimistic about the future when we realize how far we have come and where we are in the natural and repeating cycles of life.

It is not relevant to assign dates or times for the cycles. There are accounts of many other periods of peace and harmony upon this planet. It is only important to know the cycles have repeated many times. With a complete overview of the Peace Shield teachings, there is every reason to anticipate a glorious future ahead. The statement, "What used to be will be again," is a profound truth that we can hang our hats on and also store in our spiritual memory banks.

One of the purposes of this book is to reveal, through the teachings of the Peace Shield, the brightness of the light upon our beautiful path. When we understand we are finally living the events and promises of the Seventh Fire, we are unmistakably heading into the "blessedness of the First Fire." In the First Fire, people were living a full and peaceful life in harmony with all other life forms, respecting each as a relative. The people lived in harmony with all life on Mother Earth and in the universe, every direction a reflection of the Creator. In every sense, the light of the universe, the Creator's growing essence of the Great One, permeated all aspects of life - the life of the unborn, the ancient ones unseen and the lessons just beyond one's footsteps. Prayers, decisions and changes were made that were necessary for human kind to evolve closer to the eternal source of love - the Creator.

In retrospect, since the eternity of life is understood in a cyclical philosophy rather than a linear one, we spiritually developing people have much light and hope to shed upon our present circumstances. When our daily steps reflect the wisdom and knowledge of those past visionaries and prophets, every moment can be securely attached to the glorious future ahead if . . . we embrace the eternal sources of truth.

WORDS FROM THE AUTHOR

Rainbow Eagle

Not long ago, while enjoying a beautiful and sunny day on the Seneca Reservation, I was approached by Grandmother Twylah Nitsch. Grandmother is a beautiful and magnetic teacher who, at the age of 82, has made known her decision to not yet journey to other dimensions until her work and that of others is finished. She sees and fully understands this present reality, but waits impatiently to push other doors open for travel on to spirit paths. She plans every step that she makes to lead to other dimensions.

> She says, "what seems to hold the majority of people on Earth is fear, helpless negativism, lifeless energy, futility, etc. Always smile because smiling sends out a happy energy and helps to heal pent up hurt. It's healthy to smile because it releases energy that gets stuck. That's why a hearty laugh is the best medicine."

That weekend, a year before this writing, Grandmother said to me in very clear and pointed words: "You must write a book! What you teach is the real way it is. Now, prepare the young people to step into the future with those teachings." For many years I have resisted trusting the pages of a book to present the precious words of the Elders of Turtle Island I have visited. When opportunities came for me to sit with many of our Native Elders on many reservations in the U.S. and Canada, the practice of passing on teachings through oral tradition was reinforced. It is much more meaningful to teach in person, heart-to-heart, with clarity and the opportunity to answer questions. Over and over I ignored those Elders who told me, "Tell this to those who don't know. Help them to understand. Reach as many as you can. The time is right."

After years of teaching, this responsibility became more than my energy level could handle. When the teachings become a part of one's daily walk, then the need for ceremony is a natural outcome. Ceremonies to help internalize spiritual truths filled my schedule more and more. I can now understand the Seventh Fire Prophecy which said, "People will want native ways to help them survive . . . and they will not have any native blood in their veins."

As the mystery continued to unfold, I found an interesting phenomenon happening to me. Where I had previously selected the level or depth of teaching, according to each circumstance or each student, now I was pulling out all the stops. I was no longer holding back my teaching material, but letting it all come forward as if to say, "Here it is. Now be responsible with it or not, honor the Ancient Ones or not, the choice is yours."

In order for any of us to move on into other realities, changes and choices are demanded of us. Spirit called for me to relocate in northern New Mexico. In 1995 that call was confirmed during a visit to that area where I came to know the spirit of the Sangre de Cristo (Blood of Christ) mountains. My companion, Sapokni Onna, and I moved that October. We left our home with no jobs in line, no place to live and only a pick-up truck loaded with our bare necessities. This was the first move in my life that was based on faith alone. Upon our arrival in New Mexico, spirit began to guide me more and more. Then spirit said, "Write a book and begin your next work ... ."

After some 20 years of being on the Red Road (Native Spirituality), my personal vision came to me that led me to become more and more committed to the Creator's plan for me. Year after year, more life demands pointed me toward planting my steps more firmly on this spiritual and ceremonial path. Then I began to receive small, yet meaningful, "glimpses" into additional work for me to do. I was to become a participant in the journey of many truth realities that the ancient ones have hinted about all along.

Change can be both alarming and frustrating, yet when change is viewed as a natural aspect of our growth process, then awareness begins to happen. When seen as preparing humankind for new visions or realities, "change loses its sting." Wisdom keepers of the present and of the old time have already planted the seeds for us to "expand beyond our wildest imaginations".

My father would often speak of such far-out ideas as "heated side-walks, pills for food, space travel, walks on the moon" and other "Star Trek", "Jetson" realities. We kids used to be so embarrassed when his expressions got so far from the present reality. Now, at the risk of being viewed the same way, I know that there is much more light of awareness before us. We earthlings must take "a visionary look" at what lies ahead. We need only to really listen to what has already been told to us for centuries.

Let us understand more about the Peace Shield in general now. In his book, *Seven Arrows,* Hyemeyohsts Storm provides us with some information and a very interesting connection to the upcoming revelation of the Peace Shield. He mentions the existence of personal shields, men's shields, women's shields, children's shields, Peace shields and the Sacred Shields. At the time of the annual renewal, the Twelve Sacred Shields were brought together and placed around the twelve forked poles which formed the outer circle of the Sun Dance Lodge. (Note there are also twelve lodge poles around the center of the Peace Shield.) These sacred shields were never together except for Renewal time. They were never kept by any one tribe, but were passed on from one People to another.

At any one time there could be only twelve keepers of the Shields of Light. These keepers were the most powerful and respected of all the People. They were healers, diviners and teachers. It was they who carried the Sacred Shields from camp to camp and from tribe to tribe. Storm's father said, "Over the Earth there are Twelve Great Tribes. Two of these peoples are the Indian peoples". (The Peace Shield also teaches us that two of the twelve lodge poles represent Indian people - Gate Keepers). The remaining ten are other peoples of the Earth. These twelve peoples are the Sacred Shields. Storm continues, "The Chiefs Shields are tied to the Sacred Shields in that they each tell a part of the story of the Sacred Shields. There are forty-four of these Chiefs Shields. Because the Chiefs were Peace Chiefs and because these Shields were used for teaching about the Sacred Shields and the Sun Dance way, they were also known as Peace Shields or Teaching Shields". (Note: the Elder who taught me said that he was a Peace Chief.)

Storm makes another statement regarding the Peace Chiefs: "The Medicine Wheel is the very way of life of the People. It is the understanding of the Universe. It is the way given to the Peace Chiefs, our teachers, and by them to us."

So, it is with deep respect and gratitude to those who have opened their hearts to me and to the many teachers, ancient and unknown, that I say, "Thank you. I will do my best to honor the intent and spirit of your teachings."

Chapter One

VISITS WITH THE PEACE SHIELD TEACHER

I planned a visit to a small town in the upper peninsula of Michigan in the month of December. The trip itself was already like a developing disaster in the making, as snow was already over twenty inches deep in lower Michigan, and it was senseless to listen to weather reports for upper Michigan. Our destination was a small town on the northern banks of Lake Superior near the Wisconsin state line. But the trip was already planned, and there were some hearty Michlanders who were anxious to finally help me to get together with the last living Peace Shield Teacher of the Anishinabe Nation. So, disregarding the snow reports, we ventured out onto the snow-packed roads. We couldn't turn back now, as I had made these arrangements through letters and phone calls and had told the teacher, "I am coming."

Travelling behind snow plows, I had lots of time to reflect on my journeys among "Native Heritage" in the U.S. and Canada. I recalled that most of my father's known Choctaw heritage was weeded out by Indian Boarding School policy and personnel, except he spoke the Language fluently. This was a very difficult time for my full-blood Choctaw father, Henry Silas Williston. He endured the loss of both parents before he was ten years old, and was then forced to attend an Indian Boarding School. I had also experienced some

1

belittling of my "Indianness" by some non-Indian young people who had lived for some time on a reservation in the Southeastern U.S. It was often a mixed blessing to make trips such as this one because I was often led into areas where some were still working through conflicts with religious denominations that had landed on the "Res." It was understood in ancient times that one did not argue over one's beliefs. I remember an old one saying, "In all my awareness, I have not encountered warfare between Indians based upon religion . . . we honored and respected the beliefs of other tribes, and we learned how to make ourselves comfortable when we wanted to visit them."

My memories turned to times on reservations when the Elders were brought to camp to speak with the youth. Their stories, bright faces and quiet strength were apparent as they floated freely among the young people. As I continued through the snow storms, I recalled the times that the eagles came to "bless the Native gatherings in culture camps I was visiting." Surely the eagle would come to bless this visit as well, so that I could perhaps understand the teacher's broken English or perhaps be provided with an interpreter. I felt reassured, however, that I could understand this Elder when I remembered the Peace Shield teacher, Irv Romans, had presented many workshops at church and schools.

I had no picture of Irv because, up to now, he did not allow photos of himself. He had said, "I don't like my picture taken because my spirit goes with the picture. Then I have to go get it back."

2

As the snowplow continued to open the way, I thought of the recent Sacred Sweat Lodge my Native friend conducted on the Warm Springs Reservation in Oregon - such a contrast in weather conditions! When I was young, I got three honey bee stings on the bottom of my right foot. During the last round of this ceremony, I know that some three hundred honey bees found me. Afterwards, I spoke with the chief of the Washoe tribe, and he showed me how to put two tipis together to make one tipi "longhouse." Many experiences such as this held mixed blessings.

Often, after sitting with Elders for several days, they grew to trust me and expected me to pass on stories and wisdom. What would this Elder be like? I had been told that he was very anxious to see me and that he wanted to tell me all he knew. He had wisdom to share about the Peace Shield and then knowledge of healing herbs and their powers. He also spent much of his time visiting and spiritually helping a nearby Chippewa reservation. There was 98% alcoholism and 95% unemployment among these people. They were also attempting to obtain state recognition. This would enable them to limit and manage the "non-Indian fishing" off the bank of their defined settlement. Irv had commented that there was an Indian couple he prayed for often who were completing two years of sobriety, and both were employed. Though they were in their thirties, they were part of a group of elders who took on leadership of tribal affairs, and much responsibility fell on their shoulders.

The tribe was struggling with yet another issue. They wanted

3

to also recover their "Indianness." Years of hiding, being discriminated against and forced to attend Indian boarding schools were all part of the successful attempt to sever the root of Native culture. This left the community with only daily survival as a reason to rise up to each day. On my second visit, I was pleased to see that this community had pulled together to plan their first Community Pow-Wow Dance. It was especially gratifying to see parents accompany their children to be "Indian Dancers." Many adults were beginning to feel better about themselves by helping the youth to learn the traditions. Things were starting to be all right for the people again.

My own journey crossed my mind again as I remembered camping in a tipi in the cold mountains of Estes Park, Colorado. After a ceremony with some Blackfoot, I felt the heartbeat of a stone relative in my hand. I was opened to more heritage in those two days than in the previous thirty years of my life.

In the early 80's, a Klamath elder by the name of Edison Chiliquin approached me one morning at his "Culture Camp" near Klamath falls, Oregon. He told me that it was time for me to conduct the sacred Sweat Lodge. I conducted my first Sweat Lodge ceremony for him. He had such a love for young people. Edison opposed vehemently the selling of Indian land to logging companies, so he lit a sacred fire to protest the selling of the land and sent prayers about the issue. He kept this sacred ritual going for five years and refused to sell his 500 acres for hundreds of thousands of dollars.

4

Experiencing that "fire circle" with Edison was simple but powerful. It seems that he said much more by his doing than his words, which were few.

After this camp, I reflected upon a recent visit with Grandpa Foolscrow. On this third visit with this beloved Holy man of the Oglala Sioux, Grandpa took a Pipe in hand and blessed it. He then handed it to me and said, "Use this Pipe for all ceremonies for the People." He set me on a long journey of seven years preparation to be the caretaker of a Ceremonial Pipe. He was such a gentle and yet powerful man. His wife, being the "take charge" companion, took care of the groceries I brought and intently watched everything with the vision of an eagle.

My thoughts were interrupted as it was time to attend a council meeting on the reservation. Council members and a few others were discussing tribal concerns. Every once in a while, an old one would rise and place cedar on the stove to help settle the air of frustration and discouragement. I enjoyed watching the proceedings, listening to the heartfelt expressions and historical references that were all too often a part of current American Indian dilemma.

During a break, I watched an elder come my direction with a twinkle in his eye. He sat a chair next to me and spoke. "I want to tell you a story so that it will not be forgotten. The story is about when the Creator came to bring the people the drum. It was the only time that Great Manitou came to the Earth in person."

A part of this story had to do with the coming of the white man and the turmoil and chaos that occurred. "The Creator left the people with a big secret. This secret was an instrument of destruction. If the Indian people ever decided to use it, all they had to do was call the Creator and he would fulfill his promise to destroy the white man." The elder then revealed this weapon to me and said that his people have never yet called on the Creator to destroy the white man.

While in the midst of yet another Native community, I felt my heart opening to their situation of survival. They made a request for me to contact someone who could sell them a logging truck with a loader so that their tribe could begin an industry of their own. Our Indian people have endured such a long history of being kept in poverty, controlled economically, physically and spiritually, thereby blocking the building of community pride they had in days past.

Often the name of the Peace Shield Teacher was spoken by those with whom he had visited. His steadfast posture of looking to "a brighter future in the days of the seventh fire," when the people will go back on old trails and pick-up their heritage, gave them hope and endurance.

From my traveling friends I heard that a few denominations in nearby towns had invited the Shield teacher to present the Shield. This invitation would also provide an opening for him to share other reservation matters. Usually it was the women's circles who would

6

arrange seminars and speaking engagements. This leadership of feminine energy has intensified in recent years due to the sign, I believe, of the return of the spirit of White Buffalo Calf Maiden with the birth of the white calf, Miracle, in Wisconsin.

It was another such group of enlightened and visionary women who made it possible for the Great Serpent Mound in Ohio to be preserved. An old tradition tells us this was built to remember a journey of the Serpent People of the South led by the Turtle People to sacred lands in Ohio by the Turtle People. During some ten years of teaching Native American culture and spirituality, I noticed the high percentage of women in attendance. Women once again are blazing spiritual trails and now the opening of the seventh fire prophecy.

The final leg of my journey to Irv Romans was due to begin the next day. That night I found myself with a mixed-blood Indian man who appeared where I was staying. I later found out that this meeting had been arranged so that he could be around another culturally interested Native person. He was trying to strengthen his sobriety with his limited knowledge of Indian spirituality. I thought to myself, it would have been great for him to be near the Toronto, Canada area where the local AA and NA programs utilize Native spiritual beliefs and ceremonies. When I was there, I was elated to walk from some campgrounds into a primitive area where a sacred Sweat Lodge was permanently made. As I parted the hedge-like enclosure into the Sweat Lodge area, it was as if I had walked three

7

or four hundred years into the past. I gave thanks to a sensitive church denomination that provided this space year around on their campground for Native ceremony.

In my travels I also learned of another AA program that utilized Native Heritage and the Peace Shield in their recovery program. When I visited there, the workers told me that they were experiencing a 68% success rate - the highest known success rate of the Native population in the U.S. I was shown a picture of the Shield in their sharing and talking room. With all of this in mind, I was more than ready to meet with the last known Peace Shield Teacher.

Finally, the morning came, and we traveled the remaining 54 miles, disregarding the snow and weather reports of yet another storm coming. Our van pulled in front of an old brown frame house. Upstairs I could see a small bedroom that would become my sleeping quarters and "note-taking" area. After meeting Irv and his wife, he immediately took me around the house, first showing me the Peace Shield on the wood-paneled wall. Having introduced me to his living space, he sat me down on the couch saying, "You are to use the old way of learning. Learn with your heart first, then remember with your mind. As an Indian, you shouldn't take notes. Now, let's begin."

In my mind, I was thinking "I can do this; after all, he did recognized me as Native. I am ready to be a participant in this oral history tradition." But in my heart, I was panicking, for I had many

8

years in classrooms taking voluminous notes and even using a tape recorder. I took a deep breath and studied this tall, stately, gentle man in his mid-sixties. His wife had settled into kitchen chores, realizing that her husband was in for a long session of teaching.

Irv seemed to be especially excited to share with another Native person. He politely thanked those who had brought me to his home. Now, as he held the Peace Shield, he stated, "Listen, because you are going to teach this someday. The Seventh Fire is lit and all the world nations from the four races must bring their truths into the Great Lodge of the Creator." As he pointed to the blue border around the Shield, he continued, "Then there can be peace again, as there was in the First Fire. This is very important. The Peace Shield can only be taught during times of no war."

Within 45 minutes, I was emotionally exhausted. As I listened to the flood of words, I tried to organize them by assigning different truths to certain fingers of my right hand and then my left. And yet he continued, "The Creator is in the center of all things." He pointed to the center circle on the Shield. "The seven feathers tell us the seven sources of the truths. When all of the races come into the Shield, it will become a flowering tree."

Then the teachings became jumbled out of sequence as he jumped from "the first fire, to when the people had to move to preserve their heritage which was held by the elders. Finally, the people landed on an island near this homeland, and that is the

9

beginning of the fourth fire. Now the water drum could finally be sounded again. This place would be the purification of the whole world."

This was the beginning of many long hours with Irv and his wife over two winter visits. These sessions were only interrupted by my requests to "use the bathroom," where I would rush to scribble, as best I could, my disconnected and out-of-sequence memories of the teachings. Perhaps they knew of my secret, because Irv's wife always made sure I had plenty to drink so I had a reason for my "time-outs." After a while, the twinkle in her eye let me know that she was on to me.

I realized that this time I was being given the full version of the teachings from an elder. He was leaving me with a precious gift from the ancient ones.

As I contemplated more of the Peace Shield, I saw that it represented the embodiment of the temple/pyramid teaching and mystery schools. It truly symbolized the "Spiritual Lodge" of the Creator. This half-breed Choctaw had been given a birth heritage, but that heritage was significantly growing with each visit to native grandmothers and grandfathers. Could it be that they could see beyond my thin layer of Choctaw to know that I was to be a participant in the fulfillment of prophecy which calls for the sharing of Native teachings for the last time in this the seventh fire? How could I continue to think that I was only to learn from the elders with

10

no further responsibility? The circle of life teaches that "that which comes to us" must ultimately come "from us" as well. It took over four years from this time for me to fully accept my personal mission on this part of my spiritual path.

The final sign for me to share the sacred teachings of the Anishinabe/Ojibwa Nation was the coming of the second Anishinabe Elder onto my path.   After several visits to my home in Ohio, Grandfather Hollis Little Creek, who now lives in Sedona, Arizona, passed the teaching stick to me.

So now, two elders of the Anishinabe Nation had given me the honor of carrying on the truths, regardless of the fact that I was not of Anishinabe heritage.

I do not wish to debate the authority issue here. When teaching responsibility is passed on, heart to heart, without reservation, then I must respect the vision of those who walked many trails of tears for such to happen.   Many grandmothers and grandfathers have waited patiently to provide pathways of hope and joy into a bright future of the beloved Mother Earth. I can do no more than respond to this spiritual ordination to bring forth that which will once again give meaning and energy to spiritual community.

A Tribute to Irv Romans: Peace Chief/Shield Teacher

It is tremendously difficult to describe the importance of the Ojibwa Peace Shield Teacher, Irv Romans. It was not considered proper for him to speak of himself in any descriptive or biographical way. The following is my description of the life of a Peace Chief. Those who have been privileged to spend more time with him may have even more insights to share.

At the very young age of four, a candidate was taken to a Shield Teacher and left there to learn the various shields, traditions, oral histories, herbal medicines and rituals. This study amounted to the equivalent of seven degrees and usually takes fourteen to sixteen years to complete. Apprentices were taught to feel no pain except the pain of others and to stand but not be seen physically or spiritually. This involved true humility and required not taking credit for being a chosen person in the community. The gift of the Shield is a free gift from the Great Spirit. When all seven areas of the Shield are accomplished, the Shield Teacher becomes a Peace Chief. In our American educational system, it would be like having seven different degrees in theology and then becoming a professor.

The Peace Chief is the highest degree in the Sacred Lodge. He or she is entrusted with the spiritual welfare of a tribal people. His rank, however, does not entitle him to physical support or preferential treatment. Rather, he and his family eat when all others have food and are sheltered when none is in need of shelter. Shield

Teachers are the ones who make up the last appeals court when an issue cannot be settled through established means. They may not, however, take any pay for their service. Irv Romans is a spirit to be recognized and honored as the last of the 20th Century Peace Chief/Peace Shield Teachers.

"Irv" left this message to be given to the World Family. "Tell your people," he wrote, "to look back to that distant past when all people walked in a great council of harmony. The council was like a flowering tree, beautiful to see, which has now withered and died because of the darkness in men's hearts." "Brother, find your brother! Give your children paths to choose from that can't go wrong. Come together. Oh brothers, come together!"

On my last visit to Upper Michigan, I went to the same Chippewa reservation that I visited before, to honor an elder I had never met. The snow was deep, but this trip was important to me. We pulled up to the place where the elder lay in state. The place was not open, but the presence of the physical body is not essential when offering prayers for an old one. With a pouch of tobacco in hand, I left the van preparing myself for handling another loss of one of Turtle Island's elders.

My heart was full of sorrow, and my thoughts were jumbled in my head. With little emotional control, I knelt down in front of the building and lifted tobacco to the universe. I offered a prayer that this elder's life would lighten the pathways of those known to him.

13

My heart felt such pain for all of the grandmothers and grandfathers for whom no prayers had ever been offered, and I hoped that my prayers would honor them also. On that cold, winter morning, I wept tears for those not remembered. I vowed that their teachings would be carried forward so that they might live on.

I admit that for many years, the energy and motivation to step out of the crowd and travel down unknown roads to speak for the ancient ones eluded me. When I began to share, more and more my thoughts centered upon, " This was all for the elders - those who were living here and in the spirit world." All too often, they had few to learn their wisdom and stories. In some ways, I was pushed to honor my Native heritage, to fulfill prophecy and to somehow reconcile their earthly journeys.

Over many years, I became more able to place my own vision to this purpose and be more self-directed. This balance was essential for me to be able to become a resource speaker and Wisdom Keeper of Native Spirituality. After completing this task, I would be ready to step into yet another fulfillment for humanity: "Evolving into becoming members of the Universal Family."

With the passing of Irv, the reality of the responsibility of teaching the beauty paths of the Peace Shield confronted me. In the Shield teachings, Native people are to, now, in the 7th Fire, be responsible for bringing the human family together once again. What an awesome picture to behold! I now realize that the teachings must

14

go out to a greater audience than ever before. The "flashlight" of our spiritual potential can be developed into "beams of enlightenment," as humanity chooses spiritual truths and places them in their everyday walk. As the ancients have said, "Every step is sacred, every step is a prayer." Then another vision came to me that "the oldest elder passed the sage to me." This meant for me to respond by teaching the Peace Shield that had been given to me. Now I must receive this responsibility with their blessings.

I believe the time has come for Earth's people to look beyond the boundaries within which we live. As we show respect for all sources of spiritual truth, the human potential will reach new realities. We now live within a vision that ultimately will unite us with all our relations who "wait for us." It is my purpose in this writing to honor Native teachings embodied in the Peace Shield, along with all spiritual truths. This text of the ancient Peace Shield should provide the reader with an organized, easy to read text which can be used as a stepping stone toward further enlightenment.

It is also my intention, with the help of the ancient ones, to present life beyond our present limited understanding. For centuries our elders have spoken of "other life" sources. Many tribal stories or origin stories tell of beginnings far out in the universe, as well as visits to this earth reality. Our Native stories and truths present us with an expanded vision of human abilities and potential yet to be reached. "Learn with your heart first, then remember with your mind . . . now let's begin."

CHAPTER TWO

EARTH BOY AND THE SACRED COUNCIL

As a stepping stone towards the unveiling of the Ancient Peace Shield teachings, let's begin with one of the truly amazing and intriguing stories that I believe has been found in the midst of the Anishinabe people. I am grateful to those Anishinabe Elders who have called me to their side. As my father would say, "Believe it or not, it is true!" Receive this account for what it offers, use your imagination if you must, but try to place yourself within its words. Try to see in your mind the Ancient Ones as their words dance and their eyes sparkle with each picture presented. Go beyond the expressions you read, go to the secrets within the hearts of those who lead us into the great mysteries of life.

* * * * * * * * * * *

At the time, after the flood, when the second people of the Earth grew in number and their villages began to spread across the land, the second people had a very difficult time. They were a weak people. Disease took many lives each year, and sometimes a simple stumble would cause death.

Anishinabe tradition tells us that there are Seven Sacred People who are given the responsibility by the Creator to watch over the Earth's Peoples. This Sacred Council of people were made up of very powerful spirits who recognized that life was not good for the people. The Council sent a helper to walk among the Earth people and bring back to them a person who could be taught how to live in harmony with the Creation.

After six attempts to find a worthy person to bring back to the Sacred Council, the helper spirit on his 7th Journey came upon a village of people he had not seen before. He heard the village people talking about a baby boy who had just been born to a young couple; the baby was still nursing at his mother's breast. The spirit helper realized this baby was the one he was to take to the Sacred Council. The infant was innocent, his mind was untouched by the corruption and pain of the world, and he was greatly loved by the village people. He was still fresh from the Creator's side where he stayed before he came to his mother's womb. It is said that a baby cries when it is born because it still remembers what it was like to be at the Creator's side.

The helper found the baby asleep with his parents in a lodge on the outskirts of the village. His cradle-board was decorated with fine things. Truly his parents and his people must have loved him a great deal. The helper left a pouch of sacred tobacco and a piece of the child's clothing behind to show that the baby was not taken by a wild animal.

He took the baby boy to the lodge of the Sacred People, who

17

looked upon the sleeping baby. "He is too weak," one said. "He could not stand the sight of us or the sound of our voices. To do so would be fatal to him." One sacred Elder instructed the helper, "Take this child and show him all of the Creation. Show him the four directions of the Universe." The helper took the boy and did as he was instructed. It took a long time to travel so far and teach the boy so much. They traveled completely through all of the Star Worlds.

The boy was seven years old when they returned to the Lodge of the Sacred Council. The Sacred People saw them coming and realized that the boy had grown to be strong, with a mind that was sharp and curious about everything around him. The boy's heart was full of love for all of Creation.

As the boy approached the Sacred Lodge, he felt a power stronger than anything he had ever felt before. As he came closer to the Lodge, a strong emotion came over him - fear. He had felt this emotion before. The closer he came, the stronger grew his fear. Then his teaching companion, his helper spirit, comforted him.

As they arrived at the door to the Lodge, a voice rang out, "Have you brought the boy?" "Yes, I have him here with me and he is ready to come inside." With that, the door of the Lodge was opened and inside sat the Seven Sacred People. "Come in," they said to the boy and the helper. The boy noticed that the Sacred Council sat in the East - the place where he was taught the source of all knowledge and wisdom dwelled. They were dressed in very beautiful

18

clothes, and their hair was as white as snow. Their faces glowed with peace, joy and happiness.

The Sacred Ones talked to the boy in a way that seemed as though they were using their minds to send the words instead of actually speaking. The Council told the boy of how he was taken from his parents and his village and how they expected him to return someday. The first Elder pointed to a vessel that was covered with a cloth of four different colors. Each color stood for one of the four sacred directions: red for South, black for West, white for North and yellow for East. These colors represent the four races of man that the Creator placed on the Earth.

Then the Elder pulled the cloth aside and instructed the boy to look inside the vessel. It was a very quick glimpse, but inside the vessel the boy saw a beauty that he could not understand. He saw colors that had never been seen before. He saw all of yesterday and all of tomorrow. The vessel was like an opening, and out of it came a music such as the boy had never heard. All that could possibly be imagined flashed before the boy's eyes in just a short moment. Then each one of the Seven Sacred People reached inside the vessel and withdrew a gift. Each of the Seven gave their gift to the boy and rubbed it onto him.

After many years had passed, the young boy returned to Earth and travelled from village to village sharing his journey and the truths given to him by the Sacred Council. As he journeyed, he carried gifts

19

in a large bundle over his shoulder. Soon he was an old man. One day he came to the outskirts of a village where he met an old couple. The couple somehow recognized him and knew that this old man was their lost son. The memory of their son and their faith that he would someday return to them were the only things that had kept them alive for so long.

Their son, now an old man, pulled a gift out of his bundle. He then said to his parents, "I give you this gift. It represents the power, love and mercy of the Creator."

Next, the old man went to his village and told the people of his journey to the Lodge of the Great Council. He gave the people the seven gifts that he had been given from the sacred vessel and told them that certain dangers accompanied each gift. In doing so, he gave them the understanding of opposites.

Now it was time to tell the people of the Sacred Council's instructions to maintain a strong physical body. He then said that the twin of physical existence was spiritual existence. In order for the people to be completely healthy, they must seek to develop themselves spiritually and find balance between the physical and the spiritual worlds.

The old man gave the people a way to develop their spiritual growth. This way was the Vision Quest. He gave to others the ability to seek out the knowledge of the spirit world through fasting, dreaming and meditation. After using these gifts, the people were no longer diseased, and they had a sense of hope. Their hope was renewed by the retelling of the story of the old man's journey to the spirit world and the truths and gifts he brought back to them. With these teachings, the people could meet each day with the strength to journey through life's lessons.

* * * * * * * * * *

What a marvelous and insightful story from the spiritual history of the Anishinabe. Let me add that in another Anishinabe story, a boy on his vision quest traveled through the four colors surrounding the earth and thru the doorway of the crescent moon to meet with the Seven Grandfathers. The outcome of his journey was the bringing of the Sacred Sweat Lodge to his people.

All native nations have meaningful stories of personal journeys to and from the spirit world. Dream time, daydreams, visions and meditations are signs just as relevant to the native person as those which guide our daytime trails on our physical journey upon the Earth. We need to understand that occurrences in any form of reality are just as real and important as occurrences in our everyday walk of life.

In the chapters to come, I, like the one in the previous story, who has visited ancient ones, present the Peace Shield teachings. These teachings now include those teachings of all other nations represented within the blue circle of the Peace Shield. Enjoy the

21

teachings, welcome them, honor and respect them for the potential they represent. May your personal enlightened spirit be strengthened.

"I give you this. It represents the power, love and mercy of the Creator!"

Chapter Three

SOURCES OF SPIRITUAL TEACHINGS/LAWS

Oral teaching builds on a special relationship between teacher and student that often becomes a "life-long connection". There is a blending of ancient wisdom and innocence that lends itself to growth "one truth at a time". From the beginning, there must be respect on the part of both teacher and student. Respect is the basis for a meaningful relationship and the common denominator of life, as it keeps the channel open for learning to always be a part of living. Native philosophy teaches us that we exist to learn our lessons in life so that we can eventually be reunited with the Creator, where we began.

Stories which illustrate natural events in life are very effective teaching tools. In most traditions, story telling occurs in the winter months. This is a time that pushes us indoors and encourages relationships to be solidified. It is a time to get to know each other better and listen to stories to discover their deeper meanings. Story tellers can make their stories very believable. It is told that often the teller of the story actually becomes the character, even the animal, being portrayed. If told around a flickering campfire light, listeners are drawn dramatically into the tale being told.

There is a change in the dimension of the story when the teller is "an old one". Story telling is developed through years of developing imagination and listening. This is a skill that is lacking in most of us today. The listener's imagination is developed as the story is related. Story telling is an art for both the teller and the listener. The Elder sets the stage for a picture to be painted, then both participants together, using a single brush, fill in the details and choose the colors of the lessons to be taught. The beauty of the story is that the words and lessons speak to all ages of listeners in layers. One might hear one layer of a lesson at the age of four, another more complicated at the age of twelve and yet another in elder years. When the stories are repeated over and over, more depth of understanding takes place.

The creative time for learning is when minds are clear and few distractions exist for both teller and listener. Listeners, both adults and children, are very perceptive as to whether or not the teller speaks with sincerity. Likewise, storytellers are aware of the level of attention their audience is giving and if the energy and mood are right for a certain story.

An Oneida grandmother told me that any story must include two parts. First, the story is told in a way to remember a lesson or lessons. Second, the story contains interpretation or why we should remember the story. Some would use the word "moral" for the second part, but that could limit the multi-dimensional benefit of the story.

The Peace Shield teaches us that in the mid 1820's, the story tellers and interpreters of stories and drawings were given a sign that no further explanations or interpretations of stories or pictures should be given. This directive also included understandings of the pictographs on hides and cave walls and the reasons for the earthworks; fortunately, some are still around. It was during this time that the prophecy of the sixth fire told that the destiny of the red men would be out of their hands and put into the hands of those who came in the fourth fire - particularly the white race.

The Congress of the United States passed a bill at that time to "civilize" the Indian people. Appropriations were given to different denominations to go into Indian villages and obtain or destroy all articles considered sacred or powerful by the people. Grandmother Twylah described this plan as first isolating and separating the elders from the tribe, second, taking away the sacred pipe, and then taking the children away from their families to attend denominational and/or government boarding schools. In this way the intention was that the culture, history and religion of the people would be destroyed, and they could be assimilated into the white society. It was at this time "that Indian religion went underground."

To this day, there are aspects of Native spirituality that are being withheld and kept safely hidden from the non-Indian until a more appropriate time. Although the Religious Freedom Act of 1978 allows Native peoples to openly and safely practice their ceremonies, the practices are very slow to surface. This is partly due to the fact that ceremonial conductors were not able to take on apprentices for so long. And, there is also a lack of trust that remains since the fourth fire prophecy.

Grey Owl, an elder of the Oneida Nation and husband of Little Pigeon, one of my teachers, shares some memories "of the time before" the Shield. The reader will need to read beyond the words and let the truths complete the pictures he has painted:

> "Before the Peace Shield, there were only two cultures. Even before there were Indians, the Thunderbird brought this message... 'I give you the Red Road! Write it on the Earth...build sacred circles of peace, Medicine Wheels... write it in stone and wherever it can be done..."

The term "Red Road" is commonly used by most Native people of Turtle Island to mean the spiritual path or belief system which is all encompassing of life. It is a way of life that makes "every step a prayer". Often, having long hair is a Red Road symbol meaning that the person is on the Red Road or is following this spiritual path. When following the Red Road, one must care for their spiritual path as they would care for their long hair. The hair must be tended to the first thing after rising in the morning, one must be aware if it during the day's journey and then give it attention before going to bed. Some traditions braid the hair to honor and respect Mother Earth. Still others have long hair to provide the Creator with a "handle to guide them on their journey". I can now understand what was once said to me by an Elder. Holding out his long braids of hair, he said "This is our religion".

"Write it on the Earth...write it on stone". This was so that the original truths of the Earth people would always be. The interpretations would come at a later time. The sacred mounds and medicine wheels are the classrooms for learning, and the teachings are embodied in the Peace Shield as well as in other teaching shields.

Let us now discuss this ancient sacred circle of truths, the Peace Shield. It is now here for all to share and learn from. "Write it in stone..." so that the ancients may assist us to fulfill the seventh fire prophecy.

FIRST LOOK AT THE PEACE SHIELD - - TEACHINGS OF THE EAGLE FEATHERS

28

Hanging from the bottom of the Peace Shield are seven eagle feathers. These seven eagle feathers remind us of the seven ways of learning and seven sources of knowledge (teachings). The first feather (on the left) is for the teachings or the laws of Mother Earth. The second is for the teaching or laws of the Universe, sky, clouds and the above worlds. The third eagle feather is for the teachings of the North, the fourth of the East, the fifth of the South, and the sixth eagle feather represents the teachings of the West. The seventh and final eagle feather represents "the hardest way to learn"... the teachings of the Great Spirit. That which is closest to home (the Creator) often challenges us the most, calling us to sometimes relearn hard lessons over and over again.

Why are eagle feathers used as holders of great lessons? The eagle has always been thought of as the messenger from the Great Mystery to the people and vice-versa. One reason for this is the eagle's ability to fly to great heights and therefore be close to the Creator. I believe this concept of being nearer the Creator was a combination of the influence of Christianity and native belief that the Great Mystery was everywhere, even in the sky. In Native Spirituality, to think of the Creator as being somewhere "up" limits the definition of supreme love and the Creator being in all places and in all of creation. Other attributes of the eagle reflect characteristics of the Creator such as: power, beauty, skill, being in harmony with all life, ability to see into Native hearts and minds, to nurture and care for us and loyalty.

For Native peoples there is significant symbolism attached to eagle feathers. As one elder told me, "The eagle feather to the Indian is like the computer is to the white man". It "stores" many memories and powers like the computer chips. When it is used and honored in a sacred ceremony, it becomes very powerful. Certain eagle feathers are charged with certain powers and healing gifts. Always place a red cloth around them when they are stored and not in use.

Another Elder has said, "Always know where the eagle feather came from. If it is from a road kill, it must go through ceremony to be asked its journey. If there is any doubt about its purpose for coming to you, then it can cause negative things instead of positive things to happen."

Any time an animal or "winged one" gives away some part of themselves, it should be honored first before it is used. Sometimes using sweet grass will honor it until it can be taken to a proper ceremony. If an eagle feather ever falls to the ground, for example, in a Pow-Wow dance, there are traditional things to be done before the eagle feather is picked up.

Sometimes the dancer is not allowed to return to the dance area for a period of time. Other times he must make a "give away". The fallen eagle feather is always ceremonially picked up by an elder or veteran. The reason for this is that the fallen eagle feather is seen as a sign that "a warrior spirit has fallen in some kind of conflict". As a result, Native dancers will always check all eagle feathers to be

30

sure that they are secure before entering the dance arena. Only Native people have the legal right to own eagle feathers and parts. Eagle feathers are often carefully stored in red cloth, as red is a protector color. In some traditions only a Veteran/Warrior's eagle feather is to be allowed to point downwards.

REPRESSION OF NATIVE RELIGION

As we consider this topic, let us become aware of a spiritual law of the universe. When there exists a repression of significant events, spiritual lessons, people or culture, an opposite reaction will occur at some time. When these things are not honored, an even greater force or energy will surface. This principle also exists in our personal lives.

If an event or emotion is pushed back into the subconscious, it needs to be reconsidered and dealt with or it will push to the surface of our awareness. It must be dealt with and given therapeutic attention. Similarly, a real and honest effort to study history reveals many events that were "intended to be changed," as they were not in line with the philosophy of "manifest destiny". One such example was the philosophy of exterminating Indian Nations and their "savage ways". The result is the intense upheaval of positive energy, creating greater presence and interest of Indian ways than ever before the arrival of "the first boat people" from across the waters.

One might now ask, "Why is there more interest in Native

American things now? Why is this seemingly lost culture being depicted in more and more books, stories and movies?" First, prophecy foretold this happening. "...a return of the original teachings in the seventh fire." Second, this is an appropriate time for many of the man-made misconceptions about American Indians and their culture and spirituality to be cleared up and explained. I have been told that "Native people have played a part" in the leaving of some misrepresentations of their Indian ways. This was quite humorous to them. Indian people use a kind of dry humor and comical side which serves a spiritual purpose as well as serves the perspective "of the moment".

The third reason for the resurgence of Indian ways at this time is that now is clearly the time for the people to renew their respect for Mother Earth. Indigenous people all over our planet remind us of this urgent need.

Fourth, this is the time for the human family to be reminded of the spiritual idea of balance. We are in need of balancing such concepts as male/female, separation/connection, life/death, logic-mind/feeling-heart, joy/despair, hope and peace vs. the senseless futility of the presence of fear and violence.

I believe that a fifth reason for the reemergence of Native philosophy is that it is time for all people to share their truths and develop our "relatedness" as planet Earth walkers. This is the specific purpose of the Peace Shield.

32

These are some of the explanations of why many doors have been opened to indigenous cultures and spirituality. I feel much excitement about the enlightenment of our time. This excitement has been building up in my heart after many visits with the elders. Those who choose to place themselves near or within Native circles must learn from as many accurate resources as possible. When I am asked about resources, I try to be very respectful of all writers of Native teachings and culture. I usually recommend five or six books that get more clearly to the heart of teachings. Those resources which deal with ceremonies and practices can only be fully understood when there has been lengthy exposure to the culture and basic beliefs. Such understanding might take 30 - 40 years of being around native culture. I believe some of the culture and heritage is now riddled with and affected by both direct and indirect religious influences.

One must choose wisely and carefully a teacher of the Red Road. Equally important is the careful choice with whom one goes into ceremony. The seventh fire is upon us. This time has been long-awaited by the elders of many "trails of tears". With more interest in native beliefs comes the many lessons of the spiritual path which can only be compared to a "two-edged sword," and with the Red Road comes inevitable change.

If approached with sincerity, time will trim and shape one's life like a finely sharpened pair of scissors. I wish to caution those who choose to participate in native ceremonies, even on a limited basis, to be very connected to the spirit within and the sacredness of

33

all knowing. Look very closely at who is conducting the Sweat Lodge, who is leading the sacred pipe ceremony, etc. Do not expect to be invited to ceremonies that last 5-6 days in a reservation setting. Native ceremonies are powerful and especially spiritual. As Grandfather Foolscrow said, "The Creator, the conductor and the natural elements all work together."

Consider carefully the conductors of these ceremonies. Just because someone is Native or is taught by a Native teacher, does not necessarily mean that they have aligned their heart or motives with "the true spirit of Native ways". Pray about your steps on the Red Road with humility, keeping your ego in check. I don't relate this to frighten anyone. Native spiritual ways can be very beautiful, rewarding and healing. However, any true spirit path can be taken advantage of. As another Elder stressed to me, "You better know what you are getting yourself into, then spirit will strengthen you."

TEACHING OF THE TWO

Another symbol of the eagle feather is "the teaching of two". Because eagle feathers usually have both a light and dark part, they remind us that even the expression of the light has a shadow side as well. As preparation for not only understanding the Peace Shield, but also many of life's experiences, we must have a sense of the teachings of two.

In chapter eight, the reader will find a delightful creation story. In the beginning, the physical was created after a wonderful vision by the Great Mystery. The vision preceded "life and form". This duality is the manifestation of spiritual form into physical form. The Great Mystery has given us the ability to dream and also to be co-creators. If we compare ourselves to a prism through which light (gifts) travel, then we can see the colors that result as new creations radiate through us.

All creations reflect the creator's light. Native and indigenous peoples know well how colorful light can be, as one sees all creation as containing the light of the Creator. The Creator is "in everything". Looking, seeing, feeling, hearing, smelling, touching, holding, all gives first-hand experiences of different aspects of the Creator. Another layer of this concept is that to find balance, "one must look beyond what one sees, feel beyond what one feels, hear what one cannot hear..." Developing a thirst for seeing the sacred mountain as in the story of Jumping Mouse, as found in Storm's *SEVEN ARROWS*, for becoming the true-hearted eagle and having the courage to travel from one reality to another, all lead humanity to the lesson of number two.

For every action there is a reaction, for every gain a loss, for every loss, a gain... What used to be will be again. What goes around, comes around again. These are universal laws of truth. To learn one truth, another truth must be learned and then comes clarity. Contemplate some of these teachings of number two. This is just a small part , but a beginning:

1. The search for truth - the finding and utilizing of truth.
2. The Creator and the reflection of the Creator.
3. Having ownership of - the care taking of...
4. The loss of innocence - the responsibility of knowledge.
5. What is learned by victory and by defeat.
6. Success and failure.

Before discussing the teachings of two in some native ceremonies, I want to emphasize two important aspects of ceremony. One is to have a proper attitude, a good intention and a sincere reason for being around ceremony. Another is to have more than sufficient preparation before ceremony. This means to know what it's all about or at least have had teachings about a particular ceremony. Also, Native Peoples are used to preparing well in advance of ceremony with a fast, meditation, walk in nature, prayer, etc.

Now, I would like to apply the teachings of two to some ceremonies. We will not go into much detail, but I would like to touch on the Sacred Pipe ceremony, the Sweat Lodge and the Vision Quest.

In the Sacred Pipe ceremony there are two basic Native experiences. First, we must learn what to bring to us (acceptance) and then second, what to let go of (liberation). All is sacred - even that which we choose to release. That which we choose to bring toward us in the form of "the sacred breath" of the Prayer Pipe must nurture, strengthen, enlighten and empower us. That which we eliminate and expel into the air must be understood, respected, loved and released, or it will attach to us in other life lessons.

The third part of the Sacred Pipe ceremony is the balancing and respect for both male and female energies. Because the human life-form has both male and female attributes and limitations, we must recognize and accept both. The blessing of the times in which we live is that many forces are lending their assistance toward this balance.

The Pipe itself includes both male and female parts. A greater appreciation for male and femaleness is called for in the teachings of the sacred Pipe Ceremony. The stem of the Pipe contains the male energy and the bowl the female energy. From that relationship, and when each are connected forming a single sacred instrument, a spiritual/holy ritual is conceived. The Pipe further teaches us how to walk on the Red Road.

In some other Native ceremonies, the men hold the cardinal points and women hold the spirit energy in between the cardinal points. The women keep the energy flowing from point to point. Some traditions have women prepare the sacred space in which a ceremony will be held. The men will then conduct the ceremony only within that sacred space.

37

The fourth aspect of the teaching of two in the Pipe Ceremony is when "the sacred breath" of the Pipe meets with the "sacred" within us. Ceremony allows us to honor the sacredness within all life forms, and certainly we must include ourselves. We are also sacred creations of the Great Mystery.

Fifth, in a Pipe Ceremony, the Pipe Carrier in ceremony may often turn the Pipe around in a slow, circular way while holding the bowl in the left hand. When the Pipe is turned in this manner, with the bowl as the center of the circular motion, it serves as a reminder of another teaching. The center of any circle is always the spirit of the Creator. This reminds us that, to us, there is a sacred connection, a place of peace, a grounding and anchoring to the Great Mystery. This connection with unconditional love, compassion and eternal joy and peace is a needed human experience. Words cannot express this peaceful, centering connection that is possible for all of us.

A cooperative relationship is also found in some other customs connected with the ceremonial pipe. For example, in some Native customs, the pipe carrier must have a helper to light the pipe, or he must seek the help of a virgin, a child or a grandmother to help with the ceremony. For the Pipe Carrier is not to light the Ceremonial Pipe for him or herself (they are not to handle the fire). Many of the old ceremonial pipes were made four to six feet long for this reason. At that length, the pipe could not be lit by the one smoking the pipe, but had to be lit by a second person. This shared responsibility of the pipe creates a "check and balance" in Native

38

American spirituality. Having this shared responsibility keeps humility and ego in check and from interfering with spiritual intention of the ceremony.

I personally recommend there to be three to four seasoned, knowledgeable and trained people in line to serve as fire-keepers and helpers for the People's Ceremonial Pipe. This is an excellent way in which to serve the community. Pipe carriers are on call seven days a week and are to be ready at all times to serve the spiritual needs of the people, the needs of Mother Earth and even the Universe.

There are many significant lessons of two in the building of the sacred Sweat Lodge as well as in the ceremony itself. Although there are times when a Sweat Lodge is built by a group of people, even one person with the direction of an elder may do so. There is beauty in the building of the Sweat Lodge by community and in the teamwork of the Grandmothers and Grandfathers in charge. Participation by all ages, especially those who are virgins, is important to "the birthing" of the Sacred Lodge. Women and girls are directly involved in the construction of the rock pit within the lodge and the pipe-stand mound just outside the lodge. The construction of the "life-line" is entirely in the hands of the grandmothers, women and young girls. Then a grandmother and a young virgin carefully and meticulously place sage within the life-line that runs from the alter/mound into the Sweat Lodge.

More truth lessons are found in lessons given to me by

39

another Anishinabe grandfather, Hollis Little Creek. He teaches that when placing the willows of the framework into holes in Mother Earth, there should be certain prayers offered. Beginning with the Willow to the left of the doorway, and going clockwise, place each willow saying, "This is for learning, this is for doing, this is for learning, this is for doing," etc. When the last willow is placed to the right of the doorway one says, "And this is for the wisdom to do both."

The sacred relationship of two is very critical in the Sweat Lodge ceremony; some traditions call it the Stone Peoples Lodge Ceremony. The conductor of the ceremony must be spiritually in tune with the Creator, for he or she holds the doorway between the spirit world and this world. The relationship between the conductor and the fire-keeper is just as meaningful. The Elders say, "without the fire-keeper, there can be no ceremony". Often the conductor trains their own fire-keeper who may travel with them. The fire-keeper must know a great deal about traditional customs and be in harmony with the Sweat Lodge conductor. In some traditions, the pipe carrier is subject to the direction of the fire-keeper, especially when within the Sweat Lodge area. Other lessons associated with the Sweat Lodge can also be considered: 1) It is a ceremony with significance of light and darkness. 2) It is purification of both the physical and the spiritual. 3) It is cooperation between the spiritual and physical. 4) It is a ceremony that enables the Universe to respond to the needs of the individual.

40

A brief look at the Vision Quest Ceremony reveals similar lessons. When one desires to connect with their spiritual nature, it is meaningful to seek the company of the natural physical environment around them. The Vision Quest prepares one to step out of one reality and into another. This places emphasis on spiritual goals while one is attached here in the physical/material world. The Sweat Lodge then offers the vision questor the passageway to and from their Vision Quest experience.

Another relevant duality lesson of the Vision Quest ceremony is the need for both community and family support. The traditions and customs of this ceremony are conducted by sponsoring elders, but equally important is the involvement of the family who keeps a prayerful vigil throughout the entire quest. The family watches for signs, pays attention to their dreams and uses the Prayer Pipe for more spiritual insight. This balance of the community in prayer and the participant on the hill opens the door for all to be blessed and for the questor to be more fully supported and honored.

Chapter Four

PEACE SHIELD TEACHINGS

The Great Spiritual Lodge of the Creator

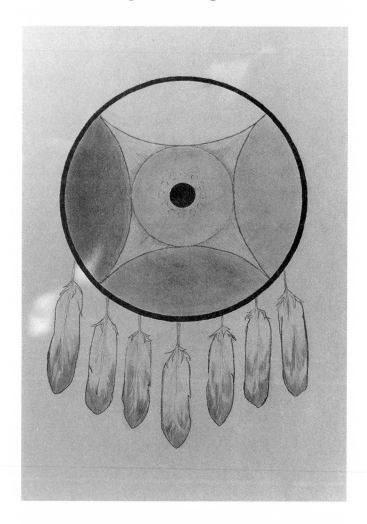

In the very center of the Peace Shield, the great Spiritual Lodge of the Creator is the constant reminder of the "great source" of life. Seeing the Great Mystery in all life and in all directions is the very first lesson of the child. The next lesson is to honor the first by saying "thank you" to the Great Spirit for fulfilling the original vision so that we can enjoy this manifestation in our material world.

The child of some cultures will be taught to honor each new day with the placing of tobacco on Mother Earth as a "thank you." With every breath, and with every use of our senses, we experience the "center of life" around us. Many hundreds of intellectual minds have tried for thousands of years to analyze and define the "nature of God." In Native thought, the Great Mystery is honored as a mystery which is experienced in everyday life, in visions, and in dreams. We earth walkers began at the side of the Creator, and our life lessons are designed to bring us back to this position.

An old story is told about "original man" who observed that all of the other creatures had mates. He asked the Creator if he too could have a mate. The Creator gave this first man the companionship of wolf. The Creator said, "Each of you are to be a brother to the other. Now both of you are to walk the Earth and visit all its places."

Original man and wolf walked Mother Earth and came to know all of her. In their journey together man and wolf became very close; they became as brothers. As a result of their own closeness, they realized that they were "brothers" also to all creation. When they had completed the task that the Creator had asked of them, they went to talk with the Creator again. The Creator said to them, "From this day on, you are to separate your paths. You must go your different ways. What shall happen to one of you, will also happen to the other. Each of you will be feared, rejected and misunderstood by the people who will later join you on this Earth."

Both the Native Americans and the wolves have clan systems and tribes. Both have had their land taken from them. Both have been hunted for their hair and both have been pushed very close to extinction. In harmony with the teachings of the Peace Shield, Native people are looking to the return of the wolf. The underlying significance of this story is in the return to closeness with the Great Mystery, the seeking to come back into the sacred Lodge of the Creator.

The blue border around the Peace Shield represents the Universal Circle of Harmony for all people in the Spiritual Lodge. The border contains all spirits who have gone before, those who walk our world at this time and those who will do so in the future. Wisdom from the Zero Chiefs spoke of the circle and the medicine wheel which are the shape of the zero. The zero is the symbol of creation. The Zero Chiefs say, "The zero is not nothing, but is instead everything." All truths and true teachings of all spiritual circles are to be included in the Great Lodge of the Creator. Further teachings indicate that his Universal Circle of Harmony becomes a

44

flowering tree.

The flowering tree holds strong symbolism within many cultures. In Native culture, the tree stands in the center of the Sun Dance Ceremony. In the Iroquois tradition, weapons of war were planted under the Great Tree of Peace. This tradition came from a vision by the Great Peacemaker. The vision of Black Elk included a flowering stick. A voice said to him, "Give them now the flowering stick that they may flourish, and the Sacred Pipe that they may know the power that is peace . . . ." Flowering Stick became the cottonwood tree - the Sun Dance Tree.

Teachings from many cultures include lessons about the flowering tree. In Black Elk's great vision, the spirits took him to the center of the universe where there was a flowering tree. In the Taos Pueblo on San Geronimo Day, the people place a sacred tree in the middle of the plaza to represent the center of the universe. In the Hindu beliefs, a sacred tree is within each individual. This tree consists of seven vibratory centers, also known as chakras. Each of these invisible chakras is connected to the spinal column. According to the Hindus, if the chakras were visible, they would look like a flower blossom. The Zero Chiefs say, "trees are called the great transformers. They possess the power to transform death. They transform the dead substance of animals and plants into life, living tissue for themselves. The number three, in the Earth's count, is the number for all plants."

Jamie Sams, co-author of *Other Council Fires Were Here Before Ours*, (the origin of the Rainbow Tree), states a similar thought. She speaks about the coming together of the five races of humans into the Lodge of the Creator:

> These two-leggeds will be called the Rainbow Tribe, for they are the product of thousands of years of melding among the five original races. These children of Earth have been called together to open their hearts and to move beyond the barriers of disconnection. The medicine they carry is the whirling Rainbow of Peace which will mark the union of the five races as one." (Seneca teaching)

The Peace Shield teaches that, except for the Human Beings, all life lives to be with the Creator and all life forms are "in perfect harmony" with the Creator. All life receives from the Creator and gives to the Creator. The spirit of the Creator is eternal and is eternally connected to the Creation. One needs only to walk in the forests, on the plains, in the mountains or among the rivers and oceans to feel the harmony among all living things. A tree is a tree, a flower is a flower, all living 100% as they are intended. Therefore, they are in "perfect harmony" with all truths and universal laws that govern this planet. A deer does not try to be a mountain lion, a rabbit does not desire to be an eagle. All of creation on the Earth, except for Human Beings, know how to live in harmony with the Creator. Only human life, or life forms that have been tampered with by human technology, have become unnatural or imperfect to the

Creator.

When indigenous people come into harmony "with the natural" through their ceremonies, the perfect reflections of the Creator surrounded their worship center. The sacred instruments used in ceremony, such as the Prayer Pipe, medicine wheel or eagle feathers, etc., reflect the love and nearness of the Great Mystery. One actually holds the Holy Spirit in their hands and places that sacredness near our own sacredness.

Each person is both a spiritual and physical lodge. The Peace Shield is a physical drawing that houses the powerful spirit/energy of spiritual truth. As the Peace Shield teacher put it, "until humans are completely in the center (in harmony with God), they must strive for balance." In our spiritual lodge, "the evil one will build his lodge where the Creator is forgotten." Only human beings have been given the freedom of choice. Thus, the earth walkers have the lesson of the number two to learn: strength vs. weakness, seeking illumination and dealing with the shadow teachings, reflecting the sacredness of the Creator without ignoring the sacredness within ourselves, etc.

One challenging lesson is that there is no "good" or "bad." One is really the mirror of the other. An effort must be made here as this may be in some conflict with other philosophies. The elder has said that life is life and its lessons are learned on or off the Red Road. If we don't learn the lesson from our journey on the Red Road, then the lesson will return to us the next time and will continue to return until learned. We always have the right to choose the life we live.

The answer to this conflict of duality is "the giveaway." The giveaway means to be in service to self and others. Yes, I did say in service to oneself as well as to the creation. All of creation reflects the sacredness that lies within each individual. In ceremony, the sacredness within each one joins with the sacredness of that around us to impact the prayers spoken.

It is believed that for whatever amount of time a ceremony lasts, the participants and the elements used reflect the divine nature of the Creator. In ceremony, "all spirits become one" to strengthen prayer.

To further understand this concept, consider the often heard pledge, "It's a good day to die." At least two spiritual concepts are expressed in this statement. One, to give fully to a chosen path of life is to be completely willing to live life to its fullest, if we have given the promise of desired companionship with the Creator. One can choose to dedicate oneself to the path with the Creator, even if it means great risk of personal harm. Second, one can more easily give fully to life when one realizes that there is really "no such thing as death." Native people describe death as only a "change of worlds." When one has a promise of complete harmony, one sees the chosen journey as one with the Creator. Peace Chief Irv said, "There is no death in the Spiritual Lodge of the Creator. An Indian never dies ... his spirit lives on in the Spiritual Lodge." The Aborigines say it this way; "Do you know how long eternity is ?"

The Peace Shield teaches oneness and unity of purpose within the center circle of the Creator's Lodge. The numbers two, five, and six have both a physical and spiritual side, as does the Creation. The number one represents the spiritual world, and the number six represents the physical world. The numbers six and one add up to the sacred number seven that is reflected throughout the Peace Shield. There are seven feathers, seven spirit blankets, seven fires, seven shells. Remember the seven sacred people who are responsible for assisting us on this Earth. Seven gifts they gave to the community by "rubbing them unto a seven year old boy". There are seven sacred ceremonies of the Lakota, Dakota and Nakota Nations. Already discussed in some detail are the seven sources of spiritual teachings.

When I sat with grandfather Foolscrow, he prepared the sacred pipe for ceremony by filling the pipe with seven portions of tobacco. These seven portions represented seven prayers to be housed within the pipe bowl. In the Seneca teachings, there are "seven worlds", seven ages on Earth through which humankind must evolve. Grandmother Twylah Nitsch shared with me that we are just coming from the "separateness" of the fourth world, called the World of Separation, into the blessings of the fifth, World of Illumination. In the Cherokee traditions, the number seven is also very sacred and meaningful. They have seven clans, a seven day creation story, and they use seven kinds of wood in their sacred fire, to mention just a few examples.

49

In some traditions, the first seven Sweat Lodge stones are honored with the Prayer Pipe as they are brought into the Sweat Lodge ceremony. I have been told that in the old days, a Vision Quest lasted seven days: three days living off the land and four days on the hill in fasting and prayer.

Here are some more sacred teachings from the Zero Chiefs. Remember that the number three is for the plants . . . the foundation of life. A three must eat light and earth. The light (number one) plus earth (number two) equals plants (number three). When any human eats a number three, he or she also ingests the earth element (two) and the light from our sun (one). Each one of us is a number five (a human). When a person is a vegetarian, then that person is a two plus three which equals five. Earth elements plus plants equals a vegetarian!.

The Dakota people have an origin story connected with the stars. The story tells that the people came from seven stars and that they were placed in the Black Hills. There were only seven tribes in the beginning, and the seven stars referred to are the Pleiades. The Creek Indians in their Green Corn dance take seven ears of corn from seven different corn fields of seven different clans. The number seven is also sacred to the Hebrews. The Menorah used in their ceremonies holds seven candles.

Before leaving this section of the teachings of the Great Lodge of the Creator, I would like to express some additional truths as they were taught to me. I believe that they attempt to create a balance with our focus on the Creator's lodge and on our own spiritual lodge. Think about them and bring other truths near to them. One truth states, "Each person has as much spiritual power unto themselves as the Great Spirit has for all people." Another says, "Often our first teacher is our own heart." And another, "As we learn, truly learn, we change, and so does our perception."

Teachings of the Number Four

As one can tell from listening to Wisdom Keepers, another sacred number is four. I have spoken before of the four levels of spirituality. At the first level, the seeker must have the opportunity to hear and consider new knowledge. Fortunately, we now live in the time of the seventh fire, which allows for greater opening to find knowledge and truth. At this time it is appropriate to remember the Native expression, "We never argue about one's beliefs."

The second level of spirituality is when we are challenged to put our learning into our walk. What value is there in the gathering of truths if they are only stored away as in a library? It is as if to say, "I have found the truth and I am saving it for sometime in the future." The energy for living out the truth is to be placed in the steps of life, rather than in the rooms of debate and discourse.

The third level directly evolves from the first and second. It calls for love of and responsibility for community. In Native life, the position of "grandfather" or "grandmother" is earned after years of experience, life observation and learning that truth is built of blocks of wisdom. We honor our elders with our purpose and respect them with our patient listening. At times, their teachings may only seem relevant to their times. We must listen beyond the obvious. Often we are being given doorways into not only the present, but the future as well.

The fourth level of spirituality is not to be spoken of or even mentioned. The elders remind us of the four good actions that we are to take in life:

1. Seek out and learn our roots.
2. Follow our vision.
3. Learn our lessons in life (respect, gratefulness, oneness with the Creator, etc.).
4. Always seek balance and harmony in life.

Within every person there is the reflection of the number four: an old man, an old woman, a little boy and a little girl. There is also the balance of age and youth, the wisdom of the grandmother and grandfather, the innocence of a child and the all-knowing of the ancient ones.

Each of us is born into one of the four directions of the Peace Shield, and we each have the gifts of that direction. The four directions of the Peace Shield also represent different times of our lives. The east represents our birth and our first perception of life. The south is our time of learning, innocence, and awareness. The west is a time of introspection and developing self worth. The north is a time of wisdom and returning to the East, our illumination of the Creator. With the guidance of these directions, we are to grow and walk the circle of harmony.

The Peace Shield teachers offer these four great predictions:
1. The destruction of life as the Creator intended us to live it.
2. The destruction of nature - the natural things that the Creator placed on the Earth.
3. The destruction of the White man's way of life.
4. Native people will once again take back their homeland and a new world will be created. Life will return to the way it was.

The spiritual teachings offered to accompany these predictions:
1. The spiritual teachings will be recovered and available once again.
2. The teachings will be learned.
3. The teachings will be practiced and used.
4. The teachings will become a part of us or rejected by us.

The Shield teacher taught that there are four great powers:

the Great Spirit, the Great Reflections (messengers), the Spirit God and the evil one.

We can now look at other teachings of the number four. There are four definitions of time: day, night, moons, and years. Four things above the Earth are the sun, moon, stars, and sky. Four parts of all living things are the root, trunk/stem, limb/leaves, leaf/fruit. The four times of our lives are baby/child, youth, adult, and elder. There are four types of creatures which live upon the Earth: those that swim, those that crawl, those that walk, and those that fly. The Sacred Prayer Pipe itself can represent four creations: Mother Earth (elements), plant (that which grew from Mother Earth), animal (the winged ones), and the human creation (represented in the making of the pipe). Finally, there are four sacred elements used in ceremony: tobacco (representing the east), cedar (south), sage (west), Sweetgrass (north). There are four spirit keepers in each of these four directions.

The Vision of Gitchie Manitou

This creation story uses the teachings of four. In the beginning, the Creator beheld a vision. The vision was then placed into a void in the Universe where the sound of the shaker was heard. Out of this nothing, the Creator made rock, water, fire and wind. Into four creations, the Creator breathed the breath of life, and the physical world, plant world, animal world and human world were formed. To each creation special gifts were given. To the humans who were the weakest and most pitiful, was given the gift of "the power to dream." Some say the gift of choice was also given. All was begun by a dream or vision, and now humans were given this same gift. Humans could manifest their dreams just as did the Creator. To all parts of creation was given the great laws of nature for the well-being of all. Following these laws would enable us to live in harmony with all creation.

A Seneca tradition says that the first creative act that manifested thought into form was the creation of Grandfather Sun, Grandmother Moon, the waters and Mother Earth. The Essence of Grandfather Sun was to give unconditional love and warmth to all who came into his circle. He also reminds each of us that we each can carry a part of the eternal flame of the Creator's love within. Grandmother Moon's purpose was to give light in the places of darkness and to reflect the light of Grandfather Sun. She also was the weaver of our feelings, making them into our dreams as we rested during the night. She manages the natural tides of the oceans and is the great weaver of the "ebb and flow" of our countless waves of emotion.

After the giving of these gifts and purposes, each part of the creation sang gratitude back to the Creator for their inheritance of beauty, wisdom, love, equality and wholeness as the breath of life was breathed into each through a sacred megis shell. Each life form had been given the ability to give and receive.

The Physical World/Creation

It is, at times, difficult to feel related to or connected to the physical creation: the stars, sun, moon and especially to Mother Earth. Native people have many ways to extend their family to include the physical world around them. These stories also add a feeling of mystery about the spirit world.

With each physical form, there is an accompanying spirit form that is in relation with the Great Mystery Spirit. For each known physical form, there is a suggestion of the "unknown forms" or realities that are just around the corner or just as near to us as the Creator's breath. This awareness of the power, the yet to be understood, is what is greatly lacking in the daily living of human beings. The readiness to see with our spiritual eyes, these not yet understood concepts that are ever-present, is somehow blocked or not developed in the typical human life. The worlds of spiritual entities such as "the little people, tree and water spirits, Big Foot, spirit guides, angels, etc.," are "mystical bridges" for humans to learn lessons from the unseen or unheard.

The stories of the elders carry a message of respect for our relationship with Mother Earth as if there were still an umbilical cord connecting us. The Earth Mother is motherhood. She births all things, nurtures all and has an abiding nature of unconditional love. The first argument given by the ancient ones to those who wished to take land was, "How can one own a piece of Mother Earth?" It seems that everything can have a price now: stones, crystals, dirt, trees, feathers, bones, etc.

Mother Earth demonstrates unconditional love to us in that no matter what is done to her, she continues to give us life. However, given that all of life is subject to the natural cycles of the Creator, Mother Earth must be true to her eternal journey, as well. When it is time to readjust her outer garments, smooth the wrinkles in her surface, realign her stressed inner muscles, or more fully purify herself for her own spiritual evolution, "all creatures, especially humans, will learn respect." We who share this sacred space must realize that we must allow her to have her own growth and development.

Our very act of breathing reminds us that what we take to our breast, we must eventually release back to the natural order of things. The ancients say that the only thing we are given "to own" is our personal physical body. We are "caretakers" of everything else. Mother Earth releases her life sustaining sacredness in the spring and summer seasons, but then goes within to replenish and purify herself in fall and winter. She washes herself through the waterways, as humans regenerate themselves through the blood veins/rivers of the physical body. When there are areas of uncomfortable tension, Earth Mother "comes alive" and moves her bone structure to re-balance and restore her physical anatomy. We must appreciate her journey, her relationship to the solar system, the galaxy and the universe. Mother Earth has a much broader and expansive mission than to just house life on her surface and within. She actively participates in her spiritual mission to evolve with all life and to ultimately give completely to the Creator's plan.

The mysteries <u>within</u> the Earth Mother have long been told of by ancient story tellers. Mother Earth is not only alive, but holds life within. Life existing below or within the center of the planet is prevalent in ancient stories. Cherokee wisdom keepers say that certain springs are door openings to the underground world. A Cherokee vision questor who wishes to visit relatives under the Earth's surface will quest near sacred springs.

There are many underground passageways spoken of that connect the eastern and western United States as well as northern and southern boarders. Those who know Native ways do not have to go far to find mystery. Mother Earth holds many "not yet to be known" mysteries that have been planted in native lore for thousands of years.

As we reflect upon the center of the Peace Shield, that which lives in harmony with the Creator, let me introduce an often misunderstood and certainly unusual creature to you. Various "Star Wars" creatures have been introduced to us on the T.V. and movie screens. Some creations, such as ET, Harry and the Hendersons and the Abominable Snowman have vicariously been made part of our culture, I believe, in part to prepare humankind for the real future to come. Native people have always known of special creatures called Big Foot, Sasquatch or Wild Man. Within such stories are glimpses

58

of giants, hairy ones, and "shape shifters" or those who have the ability to change form.

Some stories are certainly meant to be illustrations of Native truth, not at all to be taken as real or actual. All accounts of Native storytelling are intense, colorful and filled with many purposes, even if merely to "pull your leg" in a humorous kind of way. Let the reader understand, however, that there are stories which definitely reflect a very meaningful "reality" for human kind to pay very close attention to. To Native youth of ancient times, these stories prepared them for the REAL yet to come forth.

Now for the introduction to "Wildman." Other than articles about Bigfoot that I read to my sixth grade class in the sixties, I had no "close encounters" of any kind with this entity. Sometime ago, while sleeping at Grandfather Foolscrow's Sun Dance camp, however, I was awakened by the sound of cars and trucks driving recklessly through the fields of the Pine Ridge Reservation. Police cars as well were included in this chase of something. The next day, while washing my clothes at the Laundromat, I worked up the courage to ask a local elderly woman about the noises the night before. She responded, "Oh, that happens every Sun Dance. They go chasing Big Foot." Having been around ceremonies for nearly thirty years, I was aware of the presence of eagles "blessing" of ceremony, but this was the first reference to the nine to ten foot, hairy, human-like creature that often comes around certain Native ceremonies. Since this introduction, I have seen footprints and know of the presence of Bigfoot/Wildman at my own ceremonies. Occasionally, I will mention a creature called "wild man" in this book. I bring him up in this section because of Wild Man's words to us earthwalkers about Mother Earth and the natural environment.

In my teaching experiences, I have found that students of Native American spirituality often listen more attentively when I speak of Bigfoot. In the Anishinabe tradition, Wild Man spoke of his purpose and that of Mother Earth. Listen to his very sincere expressions:

> "First, you must treat the natural creation with respect. When you must come through the natural, honor those places by placing tobacco and good thoughts... Be always in wonder and awe of all the natural works that you see; they are the hand and thoughts of the Creator. These works, whether they be mountains, glaciers, waterfalls, the deepest swamps or the wildest places, (they) should never be changed, diverted or disturbed. They are to remain as they are now, just as I am to remain in my natural way..."

We owe our very lives and quality of life to Mother Earth. As receivers of this giveaway, we are obliged to love and care for her. The unborn are entitled to the same gifts of Mother Earth. The ancients made decisions only after considering the effects of their decisions upon seven generations into the future.

Native people are to honor the Earth Mother in song, prayer and heart connection by avoiding anything that would cause her harm. All ceremonies are in harmony with the elements, as well as with the energy and spirit of Mother Earth. Her life line is the water that runs through her veins, and it is vital to her existence. In ceremony, water is honored for being a precious source of our life and that of our Mother Earth. Sometimes in traditional circles, water is tenderly placed upon one's hair as a reminder of our respect for our own spirituality and the honor we must give for this element.

The Plant Creation

Teachings about the plant world will help the reader better appreciate plant life. Plant life can exist alone. Each plant was created to be self-healing. Yet, groups of plants have another power. Plants can join with others of their species to form a group or community spirit. Thus, plants can be both self sustaining and group edifying. Each valley, meadow, grove, hill or mountain possess a community mood which reflects the state of being of that place. To remove, alter or destroy a part of that place will alter the mood of that place, and the result is that it will not be what it was before.

Each species has its own complete soul-spirit that reflects the essence of the Creator. Wannabosho, a divine messenger of the

61

Anishinabe culture, says that plants possess two strong powers - the power to heal and the power to grow. Also, plants have many purposes: to sustain humans in their growth, to be medicines and to give beauty. Plants have breath, a heartbeat, they can hear us and understand our thoughts.

Wildman says, "I am to watch over those who go into the forests, swamps, hills and mountains to gather medicines and other things. If those who seek the medicine roots, bark and berries will ask me, in a good way, if their thoughts are good and if their concern is for others (their thoughts pure), I will help them to find the medicines they seek. I shall know their thoughts..."

There are special teachings and understandings about plants used in ceremony, such as sweetgrass, tobacco, cedar, sage and corn. Some of these teachings will be spoken of in the Peace Shield.

The Animal Creation

Much is written about the usefulness of the animal creation in Native stories. The Brer Rabbit stories are based on Cherokee campfire stories to teach life lessons. Four animals will be discussed from the Peace Shield. We will honor a part of the teachings of the eagle, rabbit, bear and deer.

All animals have a special relationship with Mother Earth. They have pre-knowledge of events, seasons, earth changes, and they live by the Great Laws of the natural world and even the universe. It is firmly believed that all creations reflect an aspect of the Great Mystery. Each has a form of the Creator's power and a reflection of the Great Mystery's gifts.

Since humans are also reflections of the Creator, sometimes a story character brings lessons of life a little closer. Children and even adults are familiar with Barney, Mickey Mouse, Donald Duck, Big Bird, Miss Piggy, The Road Runner, Goofy and many more. With very little stretch of the mind, one can see aspects of ourselves within each animal character. In Native times, human beings were very dependent on animals for food, clothing, tools and also for their knowledge of the world, as well as a source of knowledge about themselves. Animals also reflected images of one's character and revealed what one might be hiding in one's subconscious or not yet able to be understood. Verbena Green, elder on the Warm Springs Reservation (Oregon) spoke; "The old people used to tell me, you will learn from the animals. They will know of person you are. and they will share with you!"

The following are brief attributes of some animal creations that Native people are more familiar. Wonderful authors such as Ted Andrews, whom I have met and have much respect, and Hyemeyohsts Storm are excellent sources of animal stories. The eagle has already been mentioned.

The buffalo represents and is the great provider. The buffalo, a vegetarian, eats grass that becomes flesh. The flesh is received by the people as a giveaway. Also received is its power and energy. Buffalo meat is a sacred food in ceremony. It represents the history of Lakota spirituality. Each leg of the sacred buffalo stands for one of the ages of human kind: the rock age, bow age, fire age, and the age of the sacred pipe. The Buffalo has now given three of his legs to hold back great destruction and change for the human journey. We are now in the age of the Sacred Prayer Pipe, and the Buffalo stands on his one remaining leg (the Pipe Age). He has also given one strand of hair each year for the humans on a spiritual journey and is now nearly bald. But, the sacred buffalo remains standing to give humans time to choose the natural way to live and to return to the side of the Creator.

Coyote is a most interesting representation of many life lessons. In stories he is the only animal that can be killed and then brought back to life by another animal. Perhaps he also shows us the continual frustration with life that can accompany our path if we stray from the beauty path we are meant to travel. Even the cartoon version of Coyote depicts the futility and "no win" experiences of coyote. This animal brother never learns! To some traditions, he is the gentle and mysterious trickster. He represents all the things in life that trick us into learning.

To the Dineh (Navajo), Coyote was given control of the rain. Therefore, it was most important to respect this animal totem.

Stories about Coyote were only told after the snow fell. If Coyote crossed your path from the north or west, you needed to beware, as something was about to happen. Some Coyote stories take days to tell. One intriguing story tells of Coyote helping younger brother to learn star wisdom, and then younger brother becomes one of the holy people.

Coyote also represents everlasting life. His life force does not reside in his chest like ordinary mortals; there it could be easily destroyed. Instead, secretly he keeps one half of his force in the very tip of his tail and the other in the tip of his nose. These are the least expected places and also are less vulnerable to injury from falls and blows.

In other traditions, Coyote is closely followed by another special animal. To this animal the Creator has given the special power to restore life to Coyote when his "hard lessons" have apparently taken all life from him. This animal savior has only to jump over Coyote three or four times to resurrect him to his usual unenlightened self again. Coyote is usually referred to as "He who never learns." Native parents often remind their children, "Coyote is often a fool. By his actions with other animals, he teaches how we can see ourselves." When a child misbehaves, a parent might say, "Why did you do that? Only Coyote would do that!"

Some years ago, a vision of wolf came to me and spoke to me as he lifted himself up into my lap. He told me that my storytelling and teaching roles were spirit directed. The wolf has previously been described as a divine given partner who is connected with the human spiritual journey. We journey toward the time when all, including wolf, can again participate in sacred ceremony and community living.

In Seneca tradition, the wolf is depicted as the teacher of Earth connections. My friend and Sun Dance Brother, Dr. Chuck Ross, related a story in his book, *Mitakuye Oyasin: We Are All Related.*

> The Pte people, ancestors of the Dakota/Lakota people, had a beautiful place to live underground. They had no darkness, plenty to eat, no worries, and no troubles. A spiral cavern led to the Earth's surface. The chief of the Pte people was named Wazi, and his wife was Wahanka. Their son was called Tokahe. One day, Tokahe was wandering up the spiral cave. As he neared the entrance to the surface, he saw a wolf looking down at him. The wolf told him many tempting stories about life on the surface. Tokahe got his family and persuaded them to come out of the spiral cave to live on the surface of the Earth. Today, they are known as the Lakota people.

There are many story characters of many traditions who reflect the teachings of the Creator. They mirror the lessons to be learned with the divine companionship of the Great Mystery. All messengers of the Great Spirit reside in the center of the Peace Shield within the Lodge of the Great Spirit. Other cultures can place their notable and holy messengers within the open and growing Peace Shield.

Before leaving this section on cultural totems and significant heroes in the mystical sense, I wish to give mention of one more. In the Oglala tradition, the universe is controlled, in harmony with the Great Creator, by supernatural beings and powers. Some of these Beings desire to do good to others, intend benefit, good will and kind feelings. Others are Beings who wish to create disharmony, discord and even harm to creation. Somewhere in between these is the cultural hero, Inktomi, "The Spider."

Inktomi is sometimes known as a trickster, master deceiver or mocker. Inktomi fortunately has given culture to man and entices him out of his subterranean world. His trick is that man cannot find his way back to his underworld home. Inktomi is spoken of as both human and non human. Spider is responsible for the creation of time and space. In most stories, he finds himself traveling about the world community with animals. He is capable of transforming himself into any shape he chooses, most often that of a coyote or a handsome man. Inktomi is constantly involved in transgressions, arguments and generally illustrates undesired characteristics. Trickster stories are the favorite of young people. It is through the journeys of Inktomi that Native history and culture become known.

The Creation of Humankind

There are many Native accounts of the coming forth of the special species called man. There are many stories of man's origin from other places such as the stars, but no suggestion of the evolution theory through the advancement of another species. There is much less difficulty among Native stories and philosophy as to the blending of humanity with, or into, other species. However, to emulate or even become a bear, eagle, deer, salmon, raven etc. is a desired journey rather than something to be viewed as self degrading because of aligning ourselves with other creations.

Every life form has personal qualities that were desired and created for a purpose. Humans came into the creation picture as the last creation. Some stories refer to them as "the pitiful people" because of their difficulty surviving as easily as other creations; humans depend on the other creations to live. From their infancy, humans take longer to stand, walk, talk, and adapt. They need to be helped more than any others. It was not, I believe, the Native intent to stress the pitiful notion of humankind, as it was to emphasize the interdependency of humans to show their respect for all creation.

The Great Mystery gave very significant gifts to humans, such as the ability to dream and the freedom to choose their journey and lessons. Also given were the abilities to contemplate, meditate, think rationally and to conduct ceremony to facilitate centering and cooperation with the universe. All rituals were to establish a relationship with the rest of creation.

One story is told that after the Creator finished the creation of the physical world, plants and animals, they were told, "Learn your lessons well. You will be teaching the humans. Respect each other's differences, discipline your tongues, be responsible for your own song, talk and actions." The Creator told the water people, land families, flying people, "You will have as much power as you speak the truth."

In many ways, the Creator has instilled a sense of community and the power of the self at every point of the human's journey. There exists a purposeful and systematic progression of "divine intervention" to result in a wholeness and completeness of living standards. With each need for humankind to evolve, the Great Spirit has provided a reflection of divine spirit "through humanity" to lovingly adjust the human course toward spirituality. The organization of community and legislation, such as the Great Confederacy of the Iroquois, is balanced by the roles of the clans and the balance of male and female roles. This balance also comes through the strengthening of daily life and the planting of hope and optimism in the future.

Respect of one's personal vision was as relevant to the future of the people as was the community's role in relation to the universe. Ceremonies were systematically brought into existence by the Great Source as the spiritual need was evident. There were often many

69

distractions to the spirit path along the way, such as earth changes, special interest groups thinking themselves more important, the impact of neighboring tribes and the adoption of non-native ways to gain more material things. There have always been cracks and crevices in the spirit path that delay or divert our journeys. What causes humankind to re-evaluate, assess and finally change our course blessed the return of original truth and the teachings of the ancient ones of all spiritual circles. It takes courage to become related in a human-family way, to all dwellers and walkers on the Earth.

What is particularly encouraging is that the "length of the seventh fire" is, in human terms, substantial. The Seneca teach that we are moving into the fifth world of illumination (Seventh Fire) and out of the fourth world of separation. There are still two more worlds for humankind to experience; the sixth world of Prophecy and Revelation and the seventh of Completion. According to some medicine people of the Dineh culture, there are two worlds above this one (the fifth). The first is the world of the "spirits of living things", and the second is "the Place of Melting into One." Interesting, huh?

The creation of the human race was the last action in the cycle of life on this Earth plane. The spiritual evolution of human creation now has to go beyond the physical limitations of Mother Earth, so to speak. Many truths such as these will be more fully understood in the future. The manifestation of the symbolic "Flowering Tree" is beyond many human imaginations and realizations at this time. Until we more fully develop first, a global awareness, and second, internalize a connection with the expansion of the universe, let this stretch of our human vision become only doors yet to be opened. The beauty of life potential is mind boggling and of such proportion that we should all be excited to be alive at this time. We are getting ready for that which lays within the center of the Peace Shield and the blue circle of Universal Circle of Harmony.

Chapter Five

PEACE SHIELD TEACHINGS

Reflections of the Creator

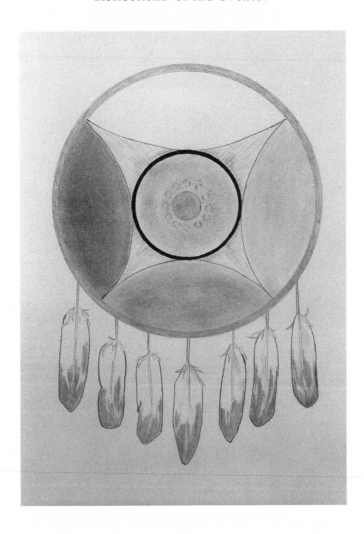

72

The second circle on the Peace Shield represents those prophets, messengers, and spiritual leaders who are the reflections or rays of light that emit the truths and glow of the Great Source/Great Mystery. These reflections include such masters as Jesus, Guatama Buddha, Krishna, Mohammed, Dalai Lama, Mahatma Gandhi, Shankara, Confucius, Quetzalcoatl, Lao-tzu, Zoroaster and a host of others. They have all brought many to spirituality.

The Dalai Lama has said, "Every major religion of the world has similar ideas of love, the same goal of benefiting humanity through spiritual practice, and the same effort of making their followers into better human beings." In the Peace Shield drawing surrounding the center within is the second circle of twelve dots. These are Spiritual Gatekeepers and will be discussed much later.

In this chapter, I wish to discuss something that more and more people are perceiving as necessary and rewarding in their lives. This challenge to all earth walkers is to become more aware of and develop respect for all religions and ways of reaching for the Creator. This is important so that there can develop more pathways which lead into the Spiritual Lodge of the Creator.

Often, those who speak with truth about how things have developed or evolved are viewed as being disrespectful. Even suggesting that things are a lot different than they were when. . .

can be deemed as negative or critical. Yet each of us must always keep our eyes open, our ears listening, our minds thinking, our hearts loving and our souls enlightened. To love the journey, walk with respect for ourselves and others, to sense the mystery of life beyond the present can open enormous and wonderful tunnels of light for each of us.

Some major church groups have historically survived by identifying a hierarchy of spiritual leaders. This is like an adoption of a royalty system that demands some level of respect of its followers. Prosperity and spirituality seem to have an expected relationship as if to say that service to others serves oneself fairly well also. One's communication skills, knowledge of the scriptures, position of attainment, and surprisingly, one's height and stature often are important assets to have. Religion is the slowest system of world orders to make adjustments in its theology and methods of conduct. It seems that at the present time, family lineage of one kind or another determines place of leadership. It is as if one is born to be or not to be something. Many of our brothers and sisters throughout the world accept this way of seeing things. Even level of knowledge and degrees determine who can speak about life matters. Those who can speak eloquently and with flowery terms have added to the surfacing of another human condition: the relinquishing of one's spirituality, responsibility to become a better person to others whom one might think are much more spiritual. Large numbers of humanity look to leadership to tell them how to come into harmony with our own Creator.

74

Having accepted this line of authority, one becomes confused by the differences between religion and the precepts of government and politics.

Native people have had some most revealing truths about what they call "the way of life" that is called religion. Only "the natural" are to be considered true reflections of the Great Mystery. Occasionally there are significant holy people or prophets who "arise from waters". They speak from journeys such as Sweet Medicine and Tecumseh. Sitting Bull spoke of his visions after prayer and fasting. Many brought great laws of life to the world after a near death experience, some have great powers, and one that I know of was born of a virgin as was Deganawidah (the Great Peacemaker). For thousands of years, Great Native Spiritual people have had powerful dreams or visions. These often came at a very young age, as happened to Black Elk (Oglala Sioux) and Plenty Coups (Crow or Absarokee).

It is known that the model of leadership for the U.S. Constitution was patterned after the great Iroquois Confederacy. One philosophy that was left out was that the Confederacy had no single leader and that all decisions were reached by consensus. Also, representation changed with every issue and council meeting. The representative from each "caucus" could only speak the consensus of the caucus and nothing else. The grandmothers facilitated the caucus, and the women had not only a vote, but a cumulative vote. If a woman was the mother of three children, her vote was considered four votes. The female population was considered the birthing and living foundation of the Iroquois nation. It was this life-sustaining energy that reached into the seventh generation. So, those involved in present deliberations had to consider the very distant consequences of their decisions. The female position of importance was not only equal to that of men, but carried a great responsibility for the birthing and care for the babies. This included not only the care of their physical well-being, but their spiritual well-being as well.

Some Native cultures did not see the need for women to participate in the ceremony of the Sweat Lodge, a purification ceremony. This was because the natural order of life gave women all they needed to purify themselves. Men, however, needed certain ceremonies to prepare them for "birthing a new journey" or a task to be done for the community.

Today, a mixture of Native people come into the Creator's Lodge. It is interesting that Native people are now challenged to practice respectful ways toward each other, just as the larger world family is similarly challenged. With most North American tribes, there is much spiritual diversity, political and cultural tension, and dependency on substances, such as drugs and alcohol.

As we make our way clearer, answers will come to us. I believe that the answers are already here waiting to reestablish the Beauty Path of Oneness. As each person, group and community of believers talk with each other, the outcome promised in many prophecies comes nearer. Unique to the Peace Shield is the bringing of a "sharing table" into the Spiritual Lodge. At this table, the human family can become aware of our neighbors.

Let this much too brief account of many of the major religions be placed responsibly into the Peace Shield. This, I believe, blazes a trail for those religions to come together into a relationship with each other. Perhaps this might only set an energy in motion that will prepare the way.

There is no selected order in the presentation of religions in this chapter. I begin with the prophet Krishna who taught people to "be humble, be harmless, have no pretensions, be upright, forbearing, serve your teacher in true obedience, keeping the mind and body in cleanliness. . ." Krishna, a prophet of the Hindu religion, probably lived before 1000 B.C. Wonderful stories are told about him, for example, the story of how he saved a countryside from a terrible storm by holding up a mountain between earth and the rain clouds. In the Bhagavadgita, the song of God, Krishna is reported to say, "Whenever there is a decay of righteousness, then I, myself, come forth,. . . for the sake of firmly establishing righteousness, I am born from age to age. . . ." This prophecy, I believe, did not mean that he himself as the same individual would return from age to age, but that God would again speak through the voices of great prophets in future ages.

77

The second prophet, Guatama Buddha, was believed by the Buddhists to be the return of Krishna. Buddha was born Prince Sidhartha, son of an Indian King of the Sakya clan or tribe, sometime in the first half of the fifth century B.C. Some movies have recently introduced "Little Buddha" to movie watchers. He was raised in luxury at the foot of the beautiful Himalayan Mountains, the highest mountains on the earth. Here he was to become a powerful king. But he left all of his luxuries and earthly powers behind and wandered in the wilderness praying and meditating. One day while he was sitting and thinking for hours under a magnificent Bo tree, God came to him in a vision. God told Sidhartha that he was to be the Buddha, the light of Asia, and one of the great world teachers and prophets. Buddha went forth among the people and began to teach them a message of love and understanding. He taught the famous "Eight Fold Way" that leads to true happiness. Studies of the life and sayings of Buddha will give only good and great wisdom.

Buddha knew that after some time, his religion would begin to loose strength and would no longer answer the new problems of the world as it should. He also knew that other "Buddhas" or prophets of God would appear to help people with new lessons. He knew that eventually a great Prophet would come who would unite all of the religions and people of the world in love and brotherhood. "I am not the first Buddha. . . nor shall I be the last. Another Buddha will arise. . . a supremely Enlightened One. . . endowed with wisdom. . . embracing the universe. . . He will be known as Maitreya. In one sense this means "The Buddha who returns is the coming of a new prophet of God." In another sense it means the "World Uniter."

Third is the Arabic prophet, Mohammed. Mohammed taught his people to "Seek help in patience and in prayer, and truly it is hard save for the humble minded...Oh, my people! Give full measure and full weight in justice, and wrong not people in respect to their goods. And do not evil on the earth causing corruption" (the Koran).

Fourth, the prophet and master, Jesus. Jesus entered the world in a Jewish body born of a virgin, not even accepted as a prophet of God by his own people. His words of truth and wisdom penetrated the most learned, his quiet actions of healing and leadership threatened the pious royalty, but the masses thronged to be near him. His many truths were spoken quietly and were directed straight at the heart and soul.

> "Verily, verily, I say unto you, he that
> believeth in me, the works that I do
> shall he do also; and greater works
> than these shall he do. (John 14:12)

Jesus gathered twelve disciples to be near him and his great teachings. He spoke of "other sheep" that he was to go to and of his return journey to humanity.

Let's look at one more obstacle to World Community. I believe it is couched to some degree in the feeling of "pride." Pride carries intense power and influence when used to lift up the memories of strength amidst defeat.

When pride brings respect to the individual and represents unwaiving faith in the Creator, this powerful attribute of assurance is most useful. When pride becomes or looks more like separation, alienation, competition or lifting one above another or one's belief or how one believes above another, then pride is being used to create the destruction of life rather than the creation of life.

A sad shadow aspect of religions is the all too frequent choice to use aggression. What can the rationalization or motivation of spiritual leaders be, to choose to battle so called "evil" forces by destroying one's belief system in the annihilation of the opposition? Too often in our planet's history, those who feared losing their power basically said to their enemy, "Because you do not think or believe as I do, you deserve to die." No amount of rationalization can justify this thinking or the outcome. Whether it is called "a threat to humanity", a crusade or holy war, fighting the "evil empire" or manifest destiny, it is still a repeat of an out of balance cycle to place more importance on one belief over another. The unfortunate result is often the transfer of hate and revenge onto the next generation, and the sleeping giant of pride is awakened to destroy and eliminate another. All groups of

80

people, including Native, know this method of never forgetting, so unfortunately, there is no room for forgiveness.

Every entity, both physical and spiritual, has an equally powerful shadow side or energy. The sun shines on all, never choosing one above another. Yet, all life has the existing presence that reflects other aspects of life as well. There is much value in the lessons of the opposite, or as Native people call, "Heyoka." These lessons can be appreciated now in stories. Therefore, we can respect and expect different truths in relation to each person as we become aware of the reflection of the Creator. The challenge lies in who is patient and loving enough to endure the World of Illumination.

In this reality, planet Earth will ultimately find her place among the stars, and we will become prepared to grow toward the reality of the Planetary Family. The Fifth World (Seneca tradition) is "going to remove all barriers to seeing and knowing all times, places, concepts, feelings, wisdom and forms without separation . . . Every life form will be able to learn and grow eternally without limitation." (Sams, Jamie and Nitsch, Twylah. *Other Council Fires Were Here Before Ours)*

Lesson of Awareness

In the Peace Shield, all life illuminates the Creator and lies equal distance from the Creator. Think of this teaching from the Peace Shield:

> Each person is a mirror to every other person.
> There is no coincidence . . .
> everything happens for a reason.

Another important lesson in Native American spirituality, after respect and honoring all life, is the lesson of awareness. In the ancient system, the Native person envisioned life's lessons as if being seen through a microscope or through the eyes of the eagle. The gift of awareness brought life as near as the mosquito or as far as the world view of the eagle; that which exsists in between was marvelously alive. There was, in life, a library of resource material, oceans of concepts and ideas to contemplate and lessons to be learned. Life was as if the Great Spirit was "sharing mystery" in one's daily journey. That which was alive begot life and then added more ingredients to life. To the indigenous people, life was as near to them as if they were their "relatives." Then it could truly be said that each being was a mirror to every other being.

However, to the child who is focused on the "becoming", the lesson, seeing the stone before stepping and falling, hearing the porcupine before it comes too close, feeling the heat of the fire before touching, smelling the bear before encountering, tasting the portions of life are lessons of awareness. The level of awareness

82

grows if the child is guided by those who have the time to share. Medicine people, those who have the philosophical and healing gifts, often spent eight to ten years living with grandparent teachers when very young. How well they learned the lessons of awareness determined when they were ready to serve the community.

Can you imagine what life would be like if your TV was constantly on, your walk was watchful of even the ants and spiders, your ears knew every sound and you were a relative to even the mountain lion? In those days, one's journey through life would be something like this picture. First you have knowledge, then you use that knowledge to honor and respect other living spaces, then after preparing oneself with thought and ceremony, one could venture into other spaces. When one knows oneself as well as other species, one can have constant guides along the way: life sign-posts, spirit sign-posts, the advice of Elders and even the dream time. These offer the life traveler ample support for their special lessons.

Taking a bold step, all spiritual teachers or teachings who have created large followings based upon spiritual concepts are to be placed in the second circle of the Peace Shield. Below follows a list of only some of them:

Christianity/Jesus, Judaism, Hinduism, Confucianism, Sikhism, Islam, Buddhism/Buddha,

Rama Krishna, Taoism, Shintoism, Jaimism, Sufism, Mohammed, Guru Nanak, Mahatma Gandhi.

It would be most delightful to place a more complete account of all the beautiful stories of the great reflections of the Creator in the pages of this book. In your own time and way, do this now so that the following story will be just added to others. Many versions of stories have similar messages, prophets and lessons. If we can sense the beauty of each way, then we can respect each as a reflection of the same and not judge one above the other. This is difficult for many because of our comfort zones with our own heritages and the amount of time spent within any given spiritual system. One of the lessons of the Peace Shield is that when there is fear, when one feels threatened by another belief, one cannot return to the side of the Creator in complete harmony. Only through faith is this journey complete. I believe, as a Peace Shield Teacher, that when we release the energy of ignorance and embrace the spirit of community and love, humanity will find the Kingdom of God.

The Morning Star Visitor

One of the first expressions of Peace Chief Irv Roman about the second circle was a story about himself at the age of nineteen. Irv had lived with grandparent teachers for about eight years and then "came out" into the world. Having the energy of a young buck, the clumsiness of the bear and the pride of an eagle, he decided to go to a church. He had learned the importance of respect for all territories, be they plant, animal or human, and therefore felt that he could be an example for his Elders and go into a spiritual community. He came out of this experience, however, with feelings of surprise, wonderment, disgust and even anger.

Before continuing Irv's story, the reader needs to understand that many Natives feel that the white race has systematically acquired Native lands and water ways as an older sibling would take from the younger. The loss of homeland, hunting and fishing lands were devastating. Even more so was the intentional removal of all articles of culture and the forced adoption of another way of life and religion. Children were even separated from their families in order for them to be more easily assimilated into white society. Many generations, including my grandparents and father, survived by hiding their heritage and going along with the military-style government boarding school/teachings. They were told what to wear, what they could and could not own, what language they could speak and what to think.

The following account by Irv Romans holds volumes of historical anecdotes that have been unknown by many American citizens. Irv came out of that church and said, " White man did it again . . . he stole another of our Indian traditions. The White people have taken our land, our fish, our children . . . now they have taken our Morning Star Visitor!"

Here now is the story of a Morning Star Visitor who came to Native people a long time ago. This story can be added to those of other reflections of the Creator in the second circle of the Shield.

In a time before the harvesting of corn, early in the morning between the false dawn and dawn, as the stars were still out, a man was seen standing up in a white canoe on the water moving toward Indian shores. The Indian people saw this and went to tell the rest of the camp. As the people waited on the shore and watched the visitor come closer, they noticed a new star appear in the sky behind him. This star had never been seen before in the sky. In that time, the people observed and knew more about the heavens than we do in this time. The Indian people called him "the Morning Star Visitor". The white canoe was moving toward them without someone paddling it.

When the white canoe reached the shore, the man stepped ashore and asked seven men to lift his canoe onto the bank. The men found that the canoe was as heavy as granite, and it took all seven men to pull it from the water. The visitor stayed and lived among the people for some time. He quickly learned their language and was soon loved by all. It was the special light in his eyes, his healing touch and the teachings he shared about how to live in the Sacred Lodge of the Creator that bonded their hearts to him. The people learned how to live in peace with all life around them. The people were happy, and even the animals yearned to be touched by the visitor.

One day, as the people gathered to listen to the teachings of the Morning Star Visitor, he announced:

"I will have to leave to go to other places. Until I return, build a sacred fire and keep it always going. This ground is sacred. I will return, and when I do, I will never leave you again. The sign of my return will be from the white mountain ash tree. Watch each spring. When the sap runs so heavy that the limbs of the ash tree bend and touch the ground, I will return."

The people were very sad that their special visitor would leave them. They understood, however, his purpose and promised to keep a sacred fire and to watch for his return. The Elders share today that since the visit of Morning Star Visitor, their ground has been sacred. It is the only place where corn can grow that far north. (The Great Lakes region) The growing season is about 110 days.

Note: There is more to this story, but this will suffice for now.

Included in Chapter eight are several more stories of a light skinned and bearded holy man who left memories in the hearts and minds of various Native people in North, Central and South America. This story is part of the original teachings of the Peace Shield. Other beautiful stories will soon be honored as well.

As a young man, Irv was blessed with the teachings of ancient wisdom. Yet, he was also angered by the loss or certainly the shared status of this special messenger. Over time, Irv recovered his posture as a Peace Chief and continued his mission to carry these teachings into the future - the Seventh Fire, and ultimately to pass those teachings from the Peace Shield on to me.

There appears to be some relationship between the story of the Morning Star Visitor and other accounts in the Americas. One such account is of a white bearded God called Quetzalcoatl, which means "feathered serpent." He was part man and part god, also named CeAcatl Topiltlin, who said that he would someday return to reclaim his kingdom.

Long ago there lived a great prophet - king of the Toltec Indians of southern Mexico. Quetzalcoatl brought a message of love and kindness and taught the people how to make new things and to raise better crops. He made the Toltecs into the greatest nation of Mexico. It is remembered that Quetzalcoatl left the Toltecs to journey to far places.

Little Pigeon, a beloved and dear Elder to me of the Oneida Nation, wrote of Quetzalcoatl in her book *Cry of the Ancients:*

Quetzalcoatl is sometimes called the Divine Lord of people of the South. There are many books written about him. Historians are skeptical of his antiquity and disagree about his origins, but the attributes of Quetzalcoatl and the belief of his followers are recognizable to the Northern Indian. He was also known to the Maya as Kukulcan and Viracocha.

A very long time ago, Quetzalcoatl descended from the sky where he had been God of the air. He became as man and lived among the people. It was said that he had been born of a virgin in a far country and had been killed upon a tree by his enemies. Then he came to the Beautiful People in his original godly form. He taught the people to come joyously to the temple with gifts of fruit and flowers. He also taught them about the obligation of man to God, of parents to children and of all to the aged. His symbol was the feathered serpent because he had power over both the wind and water. Jose` Arguelles in his book, *The Mayan Factor: Path Beyond Technology* relates, "Not just the arts, but astronomy and the calendar were affected by Quetzalcoatl, who was strongly associated with the Morning and Evening Star, the planet Venus." He left the people at last, with a promise to return and bring a time of great peace and renewal. David Freidel, Linda Schece and Joy Parker, in *Maya Cosmos* wrote, "Some legends . . . said that Quetzalcoatl had disappeared in a canoe to the east . . . ."

I have seen a photo of a mural of Quetzalcoatl and his twelve chosen followers amidst the Toltec community. There are clear similarities between the legends of the Morning Star Visitor, the Aztec Quetzalcoatl, the Hopi Pahana and Kukulcan of the Mayans. All of these cultural heroes were said to have gone to the East and promised to someday return to reunite with their people.

In this section, we need to have some acquaintance with a very unique personality known as the Peacemaker. Among the Iroquois Nation, the name Deganawidah is never spoken. He is referred to as the "Man from the North" or "the Peacemaker". Deganawidah came from the North. He was born in Huron near present day Kingston in the Canadian Province of Ontario. His nation was experiencing such a time of violence and revenge that he voluntarily left as an outcast because he had no interest in making war. It is said that he left to prove his message of peace by going in a stone canoe. Possessed with a deep and thoughtful nature, he developed a philosophy that would come to be known as "The Great Law of Peace."

Deganawidah was quite handsome, was known to talk with the birds and animals and was gifted of mind. However, he suffered a major disadvantage in a culture that valued a good speaker because he stuttered. He was born with a double set of teeth and so experienced a great deal of frustration articulating his deep thoughts. On his journey, his first convert was a woman whose house was a stopping place for many Native people. He told her to stop feeding these people and to follow the Great Laws. She did as he said, and he named her Mother of Nations. The Peacemaker connected with a charismatic Mohawk named Hiawatha who became Deganawidah's partner and greatly needed voice.

Deganawidah and his followers spent the next few years visiting and fulfilling his vision of a Great Commonwealth. The outcome was the forming of a Great League of Five Nations (Seneca, Mohawk, Oneida, Onondaga and Cayuga). The Tuscaroras were admitted as junior members in 1724. The members called themselves the People of the Longhouse. The Mohawks were the keepers of the eastern door, and the Seneca stood guard in the West. This great confederacy lasted nearly five centuries!

Deganawidah and Hiawatha wanted to take this great peace plan to all Indian people. Both looked upon the human race as one great family. They taught love, unity and obedience to the Great Mystery.

In Deganawidah's vision, he saw a gigantic spruce tree that reached up to the sky. He said,

> "If any man of any nation outside of the Five Nations shall show a desire to obey the laws of the Great Peace, they may trace the roots to their source. They shall be welcome to take shelter beneath the "tree of the long leaves" (Also call the Tree of the Great Peace).

Deganawidah also prophesied the coming of a great light from the east that would change the world. I suggest that the reader find the prophecy of the White, Red and Black serpents. Scott Person's, *Native American Prophecies* contains most of this prophecy. The Peace Shield has the rest of the story. Deganawidah said that those who gather on the hilltops were to be protected by an encirclement of fire as they renewed their faith and the principles of peace that he had established. He said that as the light approached from the east, he "would be that light, and he would return to his people . . . The Indian people would be a greater nation than they ever were before."

92

Once his vision was to be completely fulfilled, Deganawidah disappeared. It is said that he paddled westward in a canoe made of white stone. There is more to be told, but let this much be food for thought about the depth and extent of Native American spirituality. The Peace Shield once again holds a portion of these stories to be told at a later time. Perhaps this time will arrive when all religions can share and explain their truths; somewhat like placing their truths upon a potter's wheel - like placing all truth upon a turning wheel on which all truths have a place. We will all create a form that represents an embodiment of all truth. All religions have their origins in purity and in the Great Source.

The Twelve Lodge Poles

Hyemeyohsts Storm's *Seven Arrows* has made references to the Twelve Sacred Shields:

> At the time of the annual Renewal, these twelve Sacred Shields were brought together and placed inside the Twelve Forked Poles which formed the outer circle of the Sun Dance Lodge, the People's Lodge . . . The Chiefs Shields are tied to the Sacred Shields, in that they each tell a part of the story of the Sacred Shields. There are forty-four of these Chiefs Shields. Because the Chiefs were Peace Chiefs and because their Shields were used for teaching about the Sacred Shields and the Sun Dance Way, their Shields were also known as Peace Shields or Teaching Shields.
>
> The Peace Chiefs were women and men who had taken a vow to never kill another human. If a Peace Chief should be forced to kill, or was even an innocent party to the death of another human, he or she would be instantly removed as a Peace Chief and immediately made a War Chief. The War Chiefs were always represented by one woman or one man.

The information we have about the War Chiefs of old comes from the Zero Chiefs of the Ojibwa (Anishinabe) of Canada.

A similar approach was used by the Seneca Nation. All cultural information, medicines, and ceremonies were divided and taught to at least four groups. For example, four persons were responsible for a certain chapter or portion. Thus the heritage was carried four deep to ensure it would not be forgotten.

Further teachings of the Peace Shield state that the twelve lodge poles represent the twelve original peoples (door keepers) of the world. Most interesting is that two of the door keepers are Native American people. This implies that some groups would be the designated door keepers into the blessed holiness of the Great Spirit Source.

John Boatman, in his book, *My Elders Taught Me*, explains:

In the Anishinabe teachings, there are special "Passageways" which connect the Atisokanak world ("Land of the Soul - Spirits") with the Now World. The Now World persons can only use the . . . (Passageways) with the permission of Atisokanak

96

Persons. Passage into the Atisokanak world is assisted or prevented by special Atisokanak Guardians, called Doorkeepers or Gatekeepers, many of whom are powerful female beings.

I believe that the number twelve holds part of the answer to this teaching mystery. We already know of other similar references to the number twelve in religious teachings; Quetzalcoatl, Jesus, etc.

On another occasion, when I was just minding my own business, sitting in a ceremony, an Elder of Northeast Providence Ontario told me the following story:

"We have a story of when the Creator came down to the Earth. The Creator was very concerned about how spiritual ways would be carried from generation to generation. The Creator wondered who could be trusted with this mission. So, the Creator went all over the world to choose twelve men who could be entrusted to carry on the spiritual teachings. After carefully looking, the Creator selected twelve men, brought them together and spent much time teaching them. After awhile, these twelve men began to love their Creator as never before. They promised to be the Creator's messengers.

The old one then said to me, 'Hear this! Do you know what kind of people the Creator chose? The Creator chose the worst, most unhappy, sorrowful, angry and unloving people to be found. The Creator knew that by winning their hearts and minds, changing their direction in life, and placing trust in them, these twelve would never waiver. They would remain strong because of how far they had come in life to be near their Creator. They could truly be trusted to carry on the spiritual teachings to the generations to follow.' "

From the Dineh (Navajo) perspective, let me mention some brief notes regarding twelve. When Sun and White Shell Woman married, the solemn ceremony was attended by twelve male beings, twelve female beings, four rain clouds, four vapors and all the flowers of the Earth. There are twelve Holy People in their traditions. During their Dawn Ceremony, the dawn songs of the Fire Dance make an interesting prophecy:

> He is coming, He is coming,
> He is coming from the East.
> He is coming with power.

One interpretation of this chant is that the Dineh are expecting a great chief who would rise in the East wearing twelve sacred feathers. These feathers would represent his sacred principles. Under these principles, the people would unite. The number twelve is a holy number to the Dineh. It appears over and over again throughout their myths and legends. They use the twelve principles to "stay on the spiritual path. Half of them are from nature and the other half from saintly teachers."

The Zero Chiefs indicate that the number twelve is the number for all the planets: "Children, honor Mother Earth, for she birthed you and can birth all life."

My travels tell another story that tickles one's spiritual foundations. My good non-Indian friend, Chuck Maples, who lives near the Kickapoo Reservation in Kansas, related the following account of an Elder's visit to his home. It is important for the reader to know that my friend located his home near Indian people because of his love for their culture and their giftedness and potential. He began his work there as a mortician and continues to live in this small town in Kansas. It is no surprise to me that over the years of caring for Native people, Chuck gained much respect from many Elders. Due to this respect, a unique and unusual story came to him. This story was the foundation of one of the oldest and still little known religions of the Kickapoo Nation.

One evening, an Elder visited Chuck at his home, just arrived on his door step, with no need to notify Chuck of his coming. This is a way of telling if one's home and its occupants were truly open to "being a relative" as Native people see it. Midway through the evening, the Elder asked to go the bathroom. Upon his return, there appeared more of a sparkle in his eyes and a quickness to his steps. Yet, in the manner of an Elder, he waited

99

for the right moment to speak of what had been touring through the mazes of his memories of his heritage.

During a moment of non-conversation, when topics his friend wanted to cover were complete, the elder decided to open a doorway to sharing and trusting again. "He is non-Indian", he thought, "but he is a good man. I think I can again reveal a story that is precious to us. The Creator has given a sign, so it is o.k.. It is time." So, the telling went something like this:

"We have a story about the picture I saw on the wall in your hallway. A long time ago, there was so much war and fighting that no one was safe. Every where there was violence. Finally, a woman who feared for her life hid herself under the water. She breathed through a reed straw and pretended to be dead. Each day she witnessed terrible scenes of death and tragedy from under the water.

Then, on the fourth day, at midday, a figure came near her hiding place. The person's steps were on top of the water! He appeared to be very gentle and had no weapons of war with him. After pausing for a moment over her, the stranger reached out his hand to her under the water. He beckoned her to come up out of the water to make a journey with him. She raised her hand to his and left the safety of her watery hide-a-way.

Following the special visitor, she traveled many days until they came to a building of sorts. She entered a room with this man and saw twelve men waiting there for their Great Teacher. The Great Teacher began to tell of his travels and of many lessons of truth. After awhile, the woman began to cry and sob uncontrollably.

The gentle Master stopped his talk and went to her. 'Why are you crying so hard?' he asked. The Native woman said, 'You have spoken of so much beauty and wisdom, so much truth, and so many stories that are wonderful. These are things that my tribe needs to hear about and know. But, I won't be able to remember them all. I am so sad because I cannot tell my people all you have said, but only   what I can remember. I want to share all of these wonderful things!'

The Great Master then said to the woman, 'I know how you can remember these things. I will teach you drumming songs that you can sing to your people. Within these songs will be my teachings, so now you have a way to remember!'

101

The Native woman was so glad to now have a way to share the Special Teacher's wisdom with her people. She took the drumming songs back to her nation and taught them."

"Now" the elder then said, this was the beginning of our "seven drums" religion on the reservation today.

The grand old Elder went with his white friend down the hallway, and pointed to the picture of the Twelve disciples and the Master Jesus . . . the picture of the Last Supper!

Other Reflections of the Creator

Ceremony and ritual also reflect the passageway and building blocks for one to strengthen their relationship with the Creator. To Native people, ceremony was as common to daily life as it was to look to the sunrise or saying a prayer with the placing of tobacco or corn meal upon Mother Earth. From early childhood, Native children knew the nearness of the Great Mystery through their senses, dream time, their awareness of daily signs, by thinking of daily signs, stories, words of wisdom from their Elders, and their participation in and around ceremony.

From a child's viewpoint, experience with ceremony often came early. For instance, after tripping over a stone, a child's quick emotion of anger might center on the "fault" of the stone, the joke of the stone relative that hurt me. Or, maybe there was a lesson I am supposed to learn from this, but it really hurt me and made me cry, and I got so mad at the stone relative! If there was a present concern of feelings of anger toward someone, something or oneself, then a ceremony might take place to prevent lingering anger and regret. Ritual dispelled any holding onto anger or the storing of emotions, which often becomes guilt or revenge..

Therefore, every effort was made to deal with present emotional issues so that one could walk with life fully aware of oneself and all surrounding life. Emotions of remorse, revenge or disregard for self were minimal because ceremony freed one of their destructive nature. You see, the Native hunter must go into the bear's territory fully engaged in this endeavor or else suffer the consequences.

Every situation reflects the Creator's active participation in it. Even the natural "enemies" of the forest show the Great Mystery's natural law and order of things.

Let's be reminded now of the importance of being in harmony with and in connection with the natural when doing ceremony. A person doing ceremony must have more than sufficient experience and relationship with those natural elements that support ceremony. A "water pourer" (Sweat Lodge conductor)

103

for example, must not only know how to conduct the ceremony, but also:

1) know the gifts of each element
2) know how to be in cooperation with the elements
3) know how to respect the spirit of each element
4) have a strong enough relationship with each element to petition its spirit to assist in the ceremony.

One does not just grab a bucket of water, throw water on hot stones, change the form of the water to steam, without first having established a working relationship with the water, its source, and the natural cycles that made it possible for us to use it. As one can imagine, the apprenticeship to a traditional water pourer is most critical. Much time and direction is given by the Elder to train the apprentice. Some training of the apprentice includes:

1) the gathering ritual of the natural element to be used in the ceremony
2) giving proper respect to each element
3) building a Sweat Lodge prayer house
4) arranging the area of worship
5) building the sacred fire for the ceremony
6) handling the sacred elements including the sacred Prayer Pipe
7) taking charge of the Sweat Lodge area.

This represents only the first phase of the apprenticeship of the Water Pourer. The minimal requirement to partially fulfill the criteria for a Fire Keeper or Keeper of the Sacred Sweat Lodge fire is at least four to six years. This brief discussion is for the understanding that one must not only establish a meaningful relationship with the Elder and traditions, but also have a significant relationship with the natural elements and the sacred space used in the ceremonies. Not to be left out is the importance of one's own spiritual condition and family circumstance; "standing" in the community is an important consideration in being a part of the ceremony.

The previous discussion was offered to emphasize the aspect that ceremony and ritual call for much preparation, sensitivity to the natural, full understanding of the heritage and culture of a particular nation and a cooperative relationship with all persons involved in a ceremony.

It is the wisdom of the second circle of the Peace Shield that all forms of ceremony and ritual reside. All Native ceremony, such as Sacred Pipe Ceremony, Sun Dance Ceremony, Naming Ceremony, Puberty Rites, Vision Quest, etc., will not be presented here. Here ceremony, even within the same cultural circles, is often unique in its own way. To attempt to present the basic understanding of each would be most difficult.

Found within the fibers of Native culture is the respect given to one's personal vision. As is found in the Anishinabe creation story, we earth people were given the same gift that caused the Creator to put this physical world we enjoy into reality. All that Gitchi Manitou "dreamed came into being". A particular nation may have very similar protocol for how a ceremony is conducted, but there is much freedom within that cultural circle for personal vision. Therefore, there is respect for the individual dream which may at first appear to have some contradiction to the larger cultural context.

The strength of the Native culture lies not necessarily in the big picture of large gatherings, but in the well defined philosophy and spiritual foundation. Even ceremony and ritual are not the common indicator of how a nation believes.

In the old system, the Native would identify himself by first saying his spirit name. Next, usually some indication of his clan, family identity, perhaps his village or place of residence. Then, last of all, he will reveal the Indian blood that flows in his veins. For the medicine person, only the vision that directs one's purpose in the community is mentioned. In many Native cultures, the Medicine People will not speak about themselves, but will have their apprentice or spouse speak for them.

Some Historical Perspectives

In this section, it is my intention to turn back the pages of U.S. history in a rather idealistic and unrealistic way. There is great value in utilizing our imagination in "what could it have been like" as well as using our imagination to create the future to be manifested by what we do now. The combination of the two attributes, respect and awareness, contribute to the common ground, the Peace Table and the spirit of becoming "related".

There is one emotion that I have tried to cut off at the pass every time it is mentioned. All too often I hear, "I feel so guilty about what my race has done to the Native Americans," or "I feel so ashamed of what the U.S. government has done and is still doing to the first Americans. . . " The air of heavy guilt and shame are genuine feelings of many who want to finally give a degree of respect and honor to Native culture and spirituality. More and more of the rest of the story is being told. Certainly Native people know the slanted mind-set of history and archeology that has stereotyped and made indigenous people into "primitive savages."

On the other side of the coin is a number of Native people who keep placing intense feelings of guilt and shame upon the present generation which is far removed from those circumstances of history. Historical events, such as government genocide, the intentional breaking of treaties, forcing Indian people to learn white ways and the illegal sterilization of Native women by the

Bureau of Indian Affairs did happen. Feelings of anger and resentment are often justified with many reasons to "remember our heritage and Elders".

It is no surprise for me to have come across, all too often, animosities and finger-pointing at the planned actions by various denominations to Christianize the heathen, follow manifest destiny and desecrate Native Sacred belief and burial sites. I have seen many thousands of sacred objects and burial paraphernalia in foreign museums and library vaults. They are hidden from access by tribal people because museum curators fear Native groups will claim them and demand their return. In the U.S. more and more Native items are being returned voluntarily and legally. This is a very good sign. These sacred objects have great value to our medicine people today.

My challenge to Native circles and people who live with past historical pains is to look at two things. First, honor the past with the eventual fulfillment of Native prophecies. Our prophecies were given to prepare our ancestors for the journey ahead. All those who walked the paths of great and terrible times are to be honored and always given a place in our hearts and memories. Prophecy helps us to place relevance and meaning to the trails behind us.

Wisdom Keepers assist us in understanding past hurts (prophesied turns on the path) and then point us toward actions that will help us to fulfill prophecy that we are meant to do. An example of this is in the Seventh Fire or the time in which we now live. Many will go back on the old trails and pick up the sacred objects, teachings and ceremonies that were left by our ancestors. These will be brought into the Seventh Fire to be given even greater honor. In the Seventh Fire we are to go back to our Elders and seek their teachings and guidance to assist us in our Earth walk. Those Native people who continue to make room in their hearts for producing guilt and anger will find less room for participation and joy in the fulfillment of present day prophecies.

My second challenge to Native persons, who can put the past into respectful memory, is to look at who the people involved were. The people who were involved in actions toward Native people in the past 400 years are no longer living. Those who directly caused many atrocities are not doing so now. Nor can we blame a whole race of people for what only a portion of that race did in the past. Would all Native people want to be remembered for what one group might say, such as, "Indians are always drunk on Saturday night?" Would Native people want to be burdened with what one faction or group decides to do, because of family revenge or personal injustice? Let's look at who we walk with now, see beyond the institution they may represent or the ignorance they may have, because of their own people's harboring of the past.

The beauty of seeing life in cycles is that we move from one cycle to the next and gain a greater understanding and light at the end and beginning of each one. Whether a tradition calls their movement through time a "Fire", "Fifth World", "Pipe Age", "World of Illumination", etc., we are all reaching for the presence of the Great Mystery and the total fulfillment of our own sacred mission: achieving oneness. May we as Native people, Native hearted people, people of all walks of life, realize the journey before us . . . for every loss, a gain! What used to be, will be again! What lies ahead is a Beauty Path.

Some Parallels Between Red Road Spirituality and Christianity

We are all related because we all live upon Mother Earth, share the same love (gravity) of Mother Earth, the same shape/form as Earth Walkers (human), the same limitations (we have no wings, must eat three times a day, cover ourselves in winter, etc.), and we all breathe the air that the trees give to us daily. We are all nurtured by the plant world, the animal world and the water world, to be part of the whole picture. To live within the Natural Laws of Creation, we must be respectful of every part of Creation. Every part of the Creation is related to each other in some way, different and unique in some ways, dependent in some ways and yet separately envisioned. From divine purpose, from the Great Mystery and from the sacredness within us, we all are placed here on Earth to become related or not, to become

110

enlightened or not, to journey or to delay the journey to the Great Source.

The majority of persons who have been in my classes were more or less familiar with the teachings of Christianity. In this attempt to restructure the historical settings of 300 - 400 years ago when teaching was only a one-way conversation, I wanted to create opportunity for the Elders to dialog through me. Thus, there could be an atmosphere of respect and awareness to bless the exchange. The Great Mystery has given me a great deal of patience and , I believe, diplomacy to be ready for such settings. It is upon foundations such as this, my vision and my affinity to the Peacemakers such as Deganawidah, Tecumseh, Handsome Lake, the Morning Star Visitor, and the Master Jesus that have given me some edge to deal with a variety of teaching situations. Over twenty years of professionally treating personal and family mental health issues has also helped to equip me for conflict and change as well.

One of the first Native cultural experiences that helped me to see the need to facilitate communication was listening and watching a dialog between four Native Elders and some Christian theologians. This took place at the St. Paul School of Theology near Kansas City, Missouri in the early 1980's. I marveled at the great dignity of the Elders within an atmosphere of some miscommunications and lack of Native spiritual and cultural back-ground of the theologians. Yet, there was a stated willingness to

111

"hear" each other without interruption. I was amazed at the knife-cutting truths spoken so frankly and respectfully by the Elders. This dialog resulted in more education than consensus, more hearing than listening, more ridged stance than bridge building. The reason was two-fold. One reason was the time constraints that were set up by the project funding that called for specific time limits. Second was the absence of the Peace Maker spirit on both sides. Dialog was between two hard positions, each communicating deep philosophies on a surface level. On one hand was a position based on written and documented historical articles and theses. On the other, oral tradition and unrecorded historical reference provided the basis for contrasting understandings. Written histories (religious and government) were viewed as biased, slanted and incomplete. Legends, myths and oral traditions were looked at as cultural diversity, as children's stories and too simple to "house great spirituality" to compete with the major religions and studies of the land.

The outcome of this was of some benefit, however, to both groups. It was an honor to have invited the Elders, to have them listened to with respect without the threat of the theologians trying to convert them to Christianity. The opportunity to speak with much integrity was greatly appreciated, and the participation of the audience allowed for some clarification. The time constraint was the biggest obstacle for really involved dialog. More relaxed time would have helped to create more human understanding. As it was, much of the time was spent in intellectualizing by the

112

theologians and in honest attempts to inform and teach by the Elders.

With great respect and gratitude to the many Elders who have spoken in more cultural settings with more spiritual flavor, I would like to communicate as clearly as possible some of the "bridges" between two cultural religious camps. Of both camps, there are obvious generalities that could be targeted. The specifics could not fit every denomination nor be attributed to every tribe or nation's belief system. I ask the readers to view these parallels as mere building blocks that could help to create the positive attitudes which could lead to eventual and more substantial bridge building.

If you are a participant in either "camp", please sense the Peace Maker's mission; like a walk in the forest, respect our different songs, know each other's territory and yet celebrate those common pathways toward spirituality. I ask the readers of these parallels to have a sense of the many spokes of a wheel, that not only lend support to the carrying power of the wheel, but have the strong symbolism that there are many paths of spirituality leading to the Sacred Mystery.

In this section, I will give less description of Christian beliefs and more teaching of the Native. Further dialog is most welcome in the future, especially when both camps can share in a prayerful manner with celebration and thankfulness. I believe that

113

there are many more similarities than presented here, but strength develops in the coming together with honor and respect and the awareness of each other's existence in the present.

Belief in One Supreme Being

In both camps there is the belief in the one, single entity, all-powerful source, all knowing Creator/God. In most Native circles, the Great Mystery was referred to as having no particular gender identity. All ·nations had specific names for the Great Mystery which were spoken only in ceremony and never in daily conversation. As in Christian teachings, a daily walk with or relationship with the Creator/God was the ultimate goal. This relationship was to be practiced and to be improved upon with each lesson of life. For the Red Road person, the surrounding creation was of great importance in developing this relationship. One's respect for Gitchi Manitou was reflected in one's respectful treatment of the creation. Therefore, every part of creation was to be given its respectful place. With no little consideration for one part being greater or lesser, all life forms were to be viewed as "family," and all were to be equally "related" to the human creation. Mahatma Gandhi stated that one could determine the morals of a nation by the way it treats its animals. Since we are all related, this helps to ultimately develop one's desired relationship with God/Tunkashila/Wakonda/Allah, etc.

114

As a potter places one's creative spirit in all creations, the Great Source has instilled visions, purpose and a portion of the Great Light into all things in the entire Universe. To the Native, one doesn't have to look far to see/sense the Great Mystery. The Elder says, "Just take a walk in the forest, see the early morning breath of the butterflies, flowers, and stone people. The Great Spirit is so near at hand." For the indigenous people to see a reflection of God in all was a small step. They expected to hear and to welcome messages from the Creator. Historically, they never intended to communicate that they worshipped the tree, carried medicine gods in their medicine bags or wanted to become deities somehow apart from the rest of the creation. Based on inaccurate observations, written accounts of American Indian beliefs and practices often assumed belief in and the worship of many deities. These accounts were wrong. I also believe that some Native people allowed these inaccurate accounts to remain, or even planted inaccurate information to bring some sense of humor to the seemingly ridged and serious approach to religion held by most of the "boat people."

"In the beginning," one Elder said, "only Great Spirit existed." In the Western Great Lakes, American Indian Elder, John Bateman, in his book, *My Elder Taught Me*, explains that Gitchi Manitou is both the Creator and Prime Sustainer whose cosmic identity is both female and male. Bateman goes on to relate that "American Indians venerated beings other than the Supreme Being in much the same manner that some Christians

115

venerate angels and saints. These beings (manitous) were often considered guardian spirits." Therefore, both camps found the need for reflections of the Creator other than the major messengers such as Jesus, the Peace Maker, Quetzalcoatl, etc. Some Native philosophies are very complex and even difficult for the average Native person to completely understand. Perhaps this only adds to the great respect one needs to have for the mystical nature of the Great Mystery. Focus then becomes more directed toward one's self and one's final blessed relationship with the one Great Source.

Spiritual Instructions

With both spiritual groups, certain people such as Scribes - Wisdom Keepers were responsible for remembering spiritual instructions. The importance of keeping track of wisdom stories, parables and lessons that have been a part of the Great Spirit's involvement with humans is clear. On the Blackfoot Reservation, near Calgary, Alberta Canada, I was told that each tipi lodge pole was like entering a Native library through which the Elder can walk with a child. Each lodge pole represented a story, a Native truth. To the indigenous, the memory of such important events, stories, etc. was so critical to the present and the future generations (Seventh Generation) that they became life walking libraries. The average Native person exercised their memory and strengthened their ability to not only remember what was spoken, as accurate as a tape recorder, but also to mimic precisely how it was told. Wisdom Keepers and Story Tellers had many apprentices in line

116

(at least four) to carry the information into the future. I have listened to many Elders today who, time after time, speak their messages almost word for word the same way.

I have already mentioned the markings on the earth, pictographs, sacred scrolls, etc., that needed interpretation to complete their message. This required an artist, craftsman or a whole community and interpreters to remember the sacred instructions. The revelation of the Peace Shield depicts a media and manner of remembering. Unlike the usual symbol/interpretation format, it also represents a "table to be set, meal to be added to, a vision to be fulfilled." Other shields to be discovered in the future will add more color and shape to spiritual form.

Wisdom and heritage are honored in songs, hymns and musical arrangements. The previous story of the usefulness of drumming songs to the community adds sound and vibration to the memory. I have sat with one Elder of the Southwest who has the gift of applying spiritual guidance to various individual sounds and vibrations of the spoken word.

Messages hidden in sounds can provide insight into one's own vision. This Elder, Beautiful Painted Arrow, asked me to assist him in the sacred Sweat Lodge Ceremony in North Carolina a few years ago. I honor him and his vision to build peace chambers all over the world, to resonate the spirit energy of peace

117

upon Mother Earth. He dignifies the sounds of nature and those that are within the spoken word. He convinces the listener of the power and energy that is housed within vibration/sound. Music and sound are a valuable storage of power, triggers of motivation, and medicines of healing, whether in a chapel or in a hogan on the Navajo reservation.

Each time the Peace Shield Bundle is opened, song and ceremony is conducted, the Prayer Pipe is used, respectful conduct is required. The energy of the Peace Shield was brought out in a small ceremony in the Taos, New Mexico area as this book was being constructed so that its spirit could prepare the natural community and the human community for its coming. In Native ceremony there is a power in the use of objects, songs, and the drawn symbols such as in sand paintings (in healing ceremonies). Respect must be shown when in the presence of such spiritual tools.

I've mentioned a lesson told to me about the use of the swastika symbol used by Hitler in World War II. Hitler was very fascinated by Native culture, and he had every resource about American Indians he could get his hands on translated into the German language. He selected the Hopi symbol for his power symbol to be placed everywhere in his dynasty. However, as the Hopi messenger said, "He didn't know the power of that symbol . . you see, to us it means peace and harmony, but he turned it around . . . which means the opposite."

There are many who are writing about the Sacred Hoop. Some refer to it as the Medicine Wheel. To Native thinking, the Sacred Hoop houses the power of Native spirituality. Many say that when white people came into Native communities, the Sacred Hoop was broken. In recent years, I have heard more and more that many believe that the Sacred Hoop is mending. The re-emergence of Native teachings is a part of the mending. The allowing of our ceremonies honoring of Native history sends present day vibrations out that we Earth walkers have to become the Sacred Hoop. In chapter six we will add the "walk around the Peace Shield" to the many teachings of the Medicine Wheel and Sacred Hoop.

Sacred symbols and drawings are being stored in Berlin museums, and Earth works are being plowed under. In California, a major highway is being considered to run through a set of mountains that will destroy cave markings. Very little is being done to preserve these pictographs. All of these things are spiritual instructions left for humans. How long will they be present to teach future generations? Pictures of these "instructions" will not do, as the actual objects were charged with power when they are made, with prayer.

The Need for Ceremony and Worship

In both the "straight and narrow" path and the "Red Road", great emphasis is placed upon ceremony and worship. The journey toward sacred space is, perhaps, a reminder of the connection we all have to the Holy of Holies, the oneness with the Great Mystery. Various forms of worship centers are created so that a sacred place can be accessed. For traditional people, it is difficult to worship indoors in a concrete or plaster building sitting on wooden pews.

I was once arranging for some Elders to speak at a church in Calgary so that Christians could hear their views. Afterwards, a beautiful grandmother of the Carrier Nation spoke to me. "I know that the Creator is everywhere, even in this concrete and plastic. So I'm praying that I can feel the Creator in concrete and plastic." Many have told me that all you need to worship is a circle, just stand in the very center of the circle . . . that's where the Creator is.

Both camps realize the need for spiritual experience and especially spiritual renewal. Moments of full connection with the Great Spirit are often a life time memory. As I have related earlier, a young person needs to have experiences that release guilt and shame. Such forgiveness ceremonies are found in all religions. For many Native circles, the Sacred Sweat Lodge experience makes such purification possible. When one emerges from this Prayer House, they are "as a baby - clean and brand new!"

The Christian community values the need for regular worship. In the Native way, there are planned ceremonies that

120

must take place in harmony with natural events. The Hopi provide an example of this in the long line of ceremonies that must take place to "keep the Universe together and prevent the world from ending . . ." This chain of ceremony must exist in order to continue praying for all humanity.

Usually Native ceremonies occur more often when the need is apparent. There are no regular meetings taking place, but ceremony occurs as the need arises. The community gathers for as long as necessary to properly conduct a ceremony. Many ceremonies, such as the healing ceremonies of the Navajo, are quite long and involved. Such a ceremony might go on for four days and nights. Most important to this ceremony are the singers who must know more than 300 songs accurately and precisely. So important is the order and sequence of the songs that if on the third day a mistake is made, the ceremony must begin all over again.

In both communities, time, work schedules, and distance of relatives dictate the timing of services. Ceremony is usually conducted by a reverend or medicine person. Many Native Medicine people find it difficult to hold a regular job. Not many employers would support an employee who may need to leave work suddenly and perhaps not return for three or four days.

It is usually expected that some level of fasting be a part of one's preparation for Native ceremony. The extent of fasting depends on the reason for and length of the ceremony. Medicine people teach that the preparation for the ceremony is as important as the reason for the ceremony. Many years ago, I was asked to prepare for my first Sun Dance by fasting 30-40 hours every other week for six months and to also stay up all night one night a month and still work both days. I was also told to do a Vision Quest before the Sun Dance. After the ceremony, a feast is held to break the fast, and a "giveaway" takes place to honor those who have come to support the ceremony.

A personal prayer pipe is also an important preparation for the ceremony. I must remind the reader that many Native ceremonies involved extensive awareness of culture and tradition. It behooves a person to fully understand and be prepared to even attend ceremony. One must be ready to be an active participant rather than an observer. An aspect of ceremony is that each participant become "sacred" and hold their sacred energy for a good length of time. This time often involves the experience of much time in darkness, in rain, in heat, or cold and other discomforts. The preparation of fasting and prayer are therefore essential and can affect the outcome of the ceremony.

Other Parallels

Another beautiful parallel between Native and Christian religion is the belief in an eventual future including a wonderful relationship with some type of *heavenly* community. The envisioned reality of the return of Christ or the coming of Pahana, etc., brings each devoted follower to a *road of obedience* to Godly instructions. Such instructions are the road signs toward a Beauty Path, a Zion, a Kingdom. In the Peace Shield teachings, this blessedness is referred to as the Eighth Fire, or the return of the First Fire. It seems that long ago, humankind from both sides of the world (Native American and Christian) included in their belief a vision of the peaceful life. For many American Indians, there is memory of an existence of harmony and oneness that has already happened in the past. On the other hand, I should remind the reader that there is a European account of a period of 400 years known as the Golden Age.

In continuing to build a bridge of respect for Native and Christian ways, let us look at yet another everlasting truth. This has to do with the issue of life, which is one of the main roots of spirituality. There are many indications *that life is to be seen as eternal or everlasting.* Sprinkled throughout Native circles are stories of life after death. During one of my visits to the Warm Springs Reservation in Washington State, I met with a wonderful sister, Verbena Green. She and her sister were greatly responsible for the return to the heritage of her nation. She said to me: "We wait until after three days to finally bury our loved ones . . . This is because we remember a story of a woman who rose from the dead on the third day."

Other stories are of a prophet of the Paiutes, Wovoka, who brought the Ghost Dance to the Indian people in the 1880's.

123

Wovoka had a famous vision during which he lay as if dead for several days. A Seneca prophet, Handsome Lake, had a vision as his family gathered to await his last moments before death. From this came the new religion of the Iroquois which taught lessons of morality, love and concern for one another. These teachings are contained in the Code of Handsome Lake. As just a baby, Deganawidah was placed in wintry waters three times by his grandmother. Each time, however, he was found the next morning safely lying with his mother.

Today there is more openness to incidents that drastically change people's direction in life. These include near-death experiences and return from the tunnel of light. Throughout spiritual histories, one can find many "Lazarus experiences" or the return from what is called death. I remind the reader of the expression in chapter four, "There *is* no such thing as death, only the change of worlds . . ." Written upon the mind of spiritual community is the image of the Eternity of Life. Life is meant to go on and on and on . . . until, as one Elder said, "we have learned all of our lessons and return to the side of the Creator."

In American Indian lore there is an *account of a flood or deluge* that only a few survived to repopulate the Earth. The East Coast Cherokee are among those who compared their stories with Christian people. The Cherokee have a deluge story, One Supreme Being, and their sacred number is seven. They also have a Seven Day Creation story which states that their origin is among the stars.

124

An intriguing story from the Northwest, which is included in chapter Eight, could be added here. It is about the coming of the Salmon people. One could draw many parallels between the traditions and spiritual beliefs of both communities that are clearly obvious to listeners. There are some major branches of Christianity that utilize sacrifice, vows of poverty, the repression of certain sectors of our population and the discrimination of women in order to uphold tradition. In a similar vein, there are Native circles which still encourage spiritual leadership to be placed in the male population.

I believe that spirituality lives *first* in one's personal expression of truth; *second,* in the choice to find companionship with groups; and *third,* in the courage and self-discipline to walk one's talk into the next fire or dimension of existence. Try this on for size: The walk into the unknown is really into "the know" because the unknown is fully described by what has already been known. In the next chapter, what is presently unknown about the Peace Shield will be known so we can more fully prepare to travel toward the Great Mystery.

Let me state one more thing at the close of this important chapter. Some Native people are aware of prophecy that states that during this time of the Seventh Fire, the Native people of this Turtle Island must become responsible for the bringing together of the human family. Those who will be the Path Makers will be those with room in their hearts for love and respect, those who are sensitive, have knowledge and deep understanding of the heritage and who see the rainbow color of the path ahead. There are others waiting for the members of the Spiritual Earth Family to be ready for a much larger Family reunion yet to be.

Chapter Six

TEACHINGS/TRUTHS AROUND THE PEACE SHIELD

127

A glance at the Peace Shield reveals the use and honoring of the numbers four and seven. Memories flood my mind as I see as clearly as when I sat with many of the old ones as they spoke of the many truths and stories that are reflected in these numbers. Four is a traditional number, even the eagle's feet have four toes. As I listened to the elders share each lesson and experience, I could see their faces light up and their eyes sparkle.

Although looking at the Peace Shield is not the same as listening to the lessons of the grandmothers and grandfathers by the glow of the campfire, still the Peace Shield holds the energy and beauty of the many who have prayed for the wonderment of the Seventh Fire to finally come forth. It is with them that we can see each day as a lesson and each tomorrow as an open doorway into the promise of enlightenment and blessing. I now honor yet another Elder, Grandmother Louise Logan, Cherokee, as I remember her words, "One must laugh and greet each new day as a learning experience and as a special ceremony of life."

In chapter four the lessons of two were discussed. In the four directions of the Peace Shield, each animal represents our gifts and "failures", as the Peace Chief said. In other words, within each life form there lies that which strengthens it as well as that which weakens it. Medicine sisters who carefully pick the medicine roots on the Warm Springs Reservation say it this way: "You must be careful to pick the right plant that has the medicine root . . . the poison plant and the medicine plant look exactly alike, and they grow right next to each other."

The Peace Shield is a "medicine wheel." We are charged with seeking out the two aspects which lie in opposite sides of the shield. We will also see a relationship between medicine and limitation. Storm says, "the medicine wheel reveals the relationship and integration of all things created. The manner in which the medicine wheel integrates knowledge provides an easy way to learn and remember information."

Today, thanks to many who share the knowledge of Elders, there are more resources utilizing and explaining the Medicine Wheel. Truly, it is an easy way to access much wisdom and knowledge. But, an interpretation is needed.

All interpretations of all medicine wheels need not be in complete harmony. May the reader understand each "medicine" source as significant and meaningful. May the spirit of the Peace Shield quiet any mental rumblings or logical debates which could bring confusion. There can exist, for us, a peaceful interpretation of all things created if we posture ourselves as we would in the forests and woods. Let the sounds and music of life be individually appreciated, feel the vibrations that harmonize, respect the vitality of each created being. The Peace Shield intends to be like one of the conductors of a Great Symphony coming together, sometimes to be played as a chorus and sometimes as a solo melody, but always given full honor.

Let's now walk around the Peace Shield, first learning the separate truths of each direction and then the relationship each direction has with its opposite side. Another relationship of truth comes from the directions next to each other on the Peace Shield. For example, the deer person can learn from the eagle person who can learn from the rabbit person, who can learn from the bear person.

I must remind the reader again that some of the teachings are left out, or are not yet in the Peace Shield, so that other spiritual circles can bring them into the Peace Shield. This is an "open medicine" shield that awaits completion and fulfillment. Its spirit of peace and its energy of unity long to be in the hands of the complete human family. The Peace Shield's vision to be revealed in this Seventh Fire for the last time opens our own vision to be prepared for further enlightenment. We must prepare to receive medicine to restore our spiritual health, reawaken our sleeping sacredness within, to re-energize our own purposes and potential.

I also remind the reader that as we seek the teachings of each of the four directions, we encounter a door-keeper or spirit gate-keeper. Many traditions say that most of the our spirit keepers are friendly to humans. Respect is paid to them by fasting and prayer. It is to these gate-keepers that requests for teachings are made. What is not known by the journey maker, the gate-keeper will teach.

Often, the cultural "key" to admission is honoring the door-keeper by placing tobacco, which holds the request, in the fire. I visited with an Elder from the north who said that he was not yet ready for the sacred prayer pipe. He said that he "burns tobacco for the prayer request" and the completion of a spiritual "contract." When Spirit says that he is ready for a sacred pipe, he will know.

Now we burn sacred tobacco for the door-keeper of the east to release the life giving teachings. We properly request the door-keeper to send teachings to fill our void, our need to learn from the Elders. We cannot learn unless there exists an "opening" into which truth can come. To each of the four directions, Mother Earth and to our relations above, we offer and burn tobacco.

Looking to the East: The Eagle and Seven Blankets/Seats

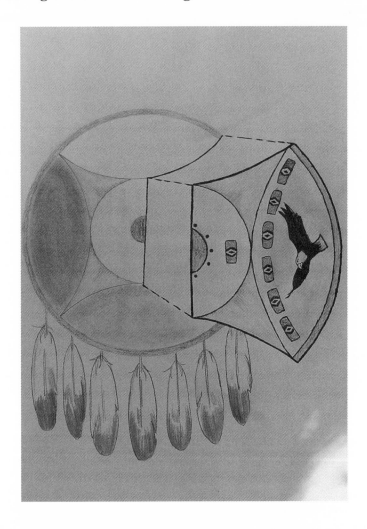

Remember the story in chapter two of the boy, taken as a baby, who received gifts from the Seven Sacred People to take back and give to his own people? These gifts came from a special and sacred vessel. Later in the story, the old man realized that the vessel was a <u>water drum</u>. Some call the water drum "Little Boy." The water drum represents all that was necessary for life. It embodied both the physical and the spiritual. The old man also realized that more knowledge would come to him with the coming of the morning sun.

So, from the Eastern doorway, knowledge flowed to him and gave him the instructions he needed to conduct the first Midewiwin (Anishinabe ceremony). On the fourth day, at sunrise, he was instructed how to construct the first water drum and what her different parts symbolized. So, the old man received his vision from the Eastern sky.

Within the water drum the old one placed sacred tobacco on the water and attached a hoop over the leather at the top of the drum. This hoop represents the sacred circle in which all natural things move. As we walk this sacred circle, we are seeking peace, harmony and oneness with all natural things. Sometime in later days, the Anishinabe attached seven small, round stones into the deer hide head. The stones represent giving honor to Mother Earth and also remind us of the Seven Original Teachings, which will be studied in the teachings of the North.

After the water drum was tied, the old one pulled a plug out

133

of a hole in the wooden vessel. He held the drum up to the Creator and blew his breath into the drum. This represented the life-giving breath of the Great Mystery which connects all life together. A drum beater was carved out of a living root. The head was carved with a curve to represent the neck of the crane and the loon.

In another story a boy was told, on his Vision Quest, how to build the first Sweat Lodge. The Lodge was to have an Eastern doorway open to the fireplace.

The east side of the Peace Shield is the color yellow to honor the morning sun. We pray that it will continue to bless us with its presence for many days and years to come. Those who are born or have residence in the direction of the East are best understood through the lessons of the Eagle. Some groups of Hopi Indians also include the red-tailed hawk as an eagle and even refer to it as the "Red Eagle."

In chapter three, great respect was paid to the significance of the eagle to Native People. The spirit of the Eagle represents that which carries our spirit to the other dimensions, a messenger to the Spirit World and Great Mystery. One should read the Eagle and the Pipe story in chapter eight. This story describes how important it is to offer tobacco each day as a thank you to the Creator. This serves as a message to the Creator that the humans are still people who sound the water drum or who use tobacco and the pipe in the proper way.

Both eagle parents feed and raise their young. The male and female energies nurture the young to develop their wings and the courage to fly into the world. For eagle people, lessons of loyalty are important and often difficult. These include loyalty to one's vision, to the Creator, and since eagles mate for life, loyalty to one's mate.

To soar with the eagle spirit can at times send us too high, too removed from present situations. The phrase, "one must be grounded," reminds us to seek centering and connection with the anchor of Mother Earth and one's own inner core. Being grounded brings us to earthly realities where we must build our nests, care for our young and teach them to respect both the Earth and Sky.

We must look at both the strengths and limitations of the eagle which are represented here in the direction of illumination, the east. The eagle can see from great distances and is able to focus on a small animal from very high in the sky. The eagle's vision is eight times greater than that of humans. This attribute allows an eagle person to narrow their vision to the pieces of the puzzle or to each step toward a goal.

But, the ability to focus on distant objects does not assure the ability to focus well on objects up close. The eagle-sighted person could be totally oblivious to their surroundings, sometimes placing oneself in a situation difficult to maneuver within as it would be when flying. The eagle is hampered by poor up-close eyesight and can become frightened when sitting on the earth and humans come

135

near. Therefore, the eagle person would rather be in a position that allows for clear observation, perhaps some distance away from where "the action is."

When teaching their young to leave the nest and fly, mother eagles will gradually lead the young near the edge of the nest as they feed them. Eagle people enjoy assisting others to see the journey ahead and even pushing the realities before others. They like to see others finally leave the nest and fly into the open skies of life.

Over a period of time eagles can develop a crusty covering over their beaks that hampers their eating. This condition forces them to land, seek shelter and protection in order to discard this obstructive build-up. Often, in the process of hammering the beak to break off the crust, the beak will break off completely and delay the thrill of the freedom of the sky until the restoration of the beak. This experience teaches the eagle person a lesson: that which provides the means for nourishment is also being affected by life's journey.

A second lesson here is that the eagle person must abandon the joys of flying and hunting for a period of time. The third lesson is the forced season of self-care which grounds the eagle to the shelter of a cliff edge or even a small enclosure such as a cave to give the proper care and energy to oneself, providing for new growth and the restoration of the tool used for nurturing.

The final lesson of the eagle person is the determination,

when it is time, to return to the sky, the life of completeness and being the eagle person they are. In early Christian mysticism, the eagle was a symbol of resurrection. Eagles are so good at getting food that they actually spend very little time hunting. It is, therefore, easy to picture an eagle spirit soaring to new heights and being in harmony with the winds and currents of life. As one of those eagle characters, these characteristics are very real to me. Another characteristic is the natural tendency to hang onto and not release what is in one's claw. The eagle has great difficulty releasing its prey and, generally, the eagle will pull and finally tear apart its fish meal. The sharp and skillful talons will snatch and hold extremely well, but the ability to release that which is in his grasp is next to impossible.

I heard a Native story that I use quite often, which illustrates this point of holding on. A little eagle was observed by an Indian boy as it took flight to snatch the salmon from a rushing mountain stream. As with many young people, the little eagle had envisioned himself catching a very large salmon and lifting it out of the water and to the shore. All the other little eagles would envy him, and the elders would be so proud of his success.

Having dreamed this, the little eagle waited patiently for the largest salmon to come his way. Being so patient was very difficult for such a young hearted one. Finally, he sighted a very large salmon from afar. After circling to position his approach, the little eagle began his calculated descent. With perfect timing, he swooped down and caught the salmon in both talons.

"A good catch with such beauty and skill" he thinks to himself. However, the Native boy saw a very sad thing that day. The salmon was too big for the little eagle to raise out of the water even with his powerful wings. The little eagle could not release the heavy weight attached to his talons. The salmon thrashed from side to side to free itself, but the talons grasped tighter and tighter around him. The little eagle went to a watery death as he was pulled under the water by the very food he sought because he could not release his prey in time to escape this life-changing journey.

The eagle has not only a sharp beak, but also powerfully strong jaw muscles. Eagle people must know when to speak, how much to say and how strongly to state their ideas and opinions. It is said that the ears of the eagle hear very well. The eagle hunts as much by ear as by sight. The hearing of eagle people is an important part of their spiritual and their physical world.

The mating ritual of the eagle reflects the mystical joy, danger, excitement and power of sexual energy. Eagles mate as they fly or even fall and plunge into deep dives. People with eagle energy must properly manage their sexual energies so that they can open to new heights and conditions conducive to flight rather than to devastating falls.

Eagles are also given many attributes that assist them to know and understand themselves and others. To accept the eagle medicine, one must take on the responsibilities and power of becoming much more than one now appears to be. One must accept increased responsibility for spiritual growth, touch and observe all life with healing. Eagle feathers are often used as tools for healing.

Some of the limitations or failures of eagle people include; the need to go within, caring for self, the need to remain grounded, poor sight up close, the need to learn to let go or release, the need to discipline one's tongue and the management of its flying joys. There is another failure that the Peace Chief pointed out to me. The eagle is inclined to be a glutton. This tendency to eat more than necessary is just another indicator of living life to its fullest. Eagles known as "snake eagle" swallow the snake whole partly due to the fact that their toes are short and strong and they are unable to hold onto wiggling snakes.

The Seven Original Clan Seats/Blankets

As with the eco systems that keep the life of nature in balance, so also the human community must be adequately fashioned to give its members a sense of harmony and consistency. Many historical observations of authors writing about Native communities tell of loving and peaceful people within well integrated governmental systems. This section of the Peace Shield attempts to highlight this "structured environment" that has been the backbone of Native heritage. An example is the Great Iroquois Confederacy.

One must keep in mind that when there are expressions of the obvious facts, such as those taught in this book of the Peace Shield, there is always another reflection. Along with the told and explained that the Elders choose to reveal is the unexplained, the "hidden," and the secrets that can be found in the lightening flashed of their eyes. Later events and truths tell the rest of the story that was once disguised within their stories.

Within the teachings to follow are such yet-to-be-fully understood truths. My prayer is that the reader will have the patience and courage to assist in the unveiling and the fulfillment of the teachings, symbolized in this ancient yet futuristic Peace Shield.

We now proceed to one model of many Native community models that were designed to facilitate both personal and tribal spiritual strength and development. Much respect is paid in advance to the other models of tribal organization that will be brought into the Spiritual Lodge of the Creator.

Among the Anishinabe Peoples, it is told that the Creator decided that they needed a system of government to give them strength and order. The people were given the seven original clan system. Each clan was given a specific way to serve the community.

The power and responsibility of leadership was given to the Crane and Loon clans. Remember the drum beater carved by the Old one. Those in these two clans were born with natural qualities for leadership and each checked on the other.

140

The Fish Clan, or sometimes called the Water Clan, stood between the Crane and Loon Clans. They were the intellectuals, sometimes called the "star gazers." They were known for their constant pursuit of meditation and philosophy. The Fish Clan would settle disputes between the Crane and Loon Clans if a deciding vote was needed. The turtle was the head of the Fish Clan. The attributes of meekness and humility coupled with quick and sharp minds, plus, no doubt, the vision of "peace keepers," gave members of the Fish clan Wisdom-Keeper status.

Among my Choctaw heritage, the Women's Circle was the means of intervention when the nation was not in line with long-term vision and energy that was to nurture the coming generations. The Choctaw women Elders decided if a leader needed to be impeached, even if the whole tribe had voted the leader in.

The Fish Clan balanced their blessed memories with one foot in the "here and now" and the other in the world to come. Their meditations provided opportunity to envision the future and for the spirit world to be a part of the decisions of the present. This is unlike the present intervention by the U.S. Supreme Court which bases decisions on past litigations rather than building pathways for the yet-to be born. This is like having to remove mountains of barriers first before blazing the trails toward advancement and enlightenment.

The Bear Clan served the community as protection so that everyday life would be free from outside distraction. Bear Clan

141

members spent most of their time patrolling the outskirts of the village. Because they spent much time in the outdoors, the members also became herbalists. Their knowledge of plants and roots provided medicines to treat illnesses of the community. Members of the Bear Clan were also stationed at the east door of the Midiwiwin Lodge ceremonies.

As will be seen later in the teachings of the West, the Bear power is the guardian of many secret cures. The Northern Lights are the intensifiers/amplifiers of the Bear power. The teachings of the West on the Peace Shield balance/penetrate the darkness or shadow lessons of the East; the beauty and light (knowledge) of the East will balance the lessons learned in the West. The teachings will also reveal that the "sees afar" visioning or the need to go within and meditate gives balance to the attributes across the Peace Shield.

The Martin Clan would be known today as the War Chiefs or Warriors. They are the protectors and defenders of the village at all costs. In the Choctaw heritage, a separate and special village was designated to this clan. Their commitment was to balance between their personal vision and their total giveaway to community and heritage. Their level of spirituality was equal to the rest of the community, but their focus was directed toward one aspect of community life. This focus was the readiness, energy and cooperation for battle. Because there were few identified leaders, each member was a master of strategy and was committed to the belief that all life is to be given totally in the "living" and "giving" of

142

life. In battle each person had the option to fulfill both personal and squadron missions and visions.

There is a story about a time when the Warrior Clan became too forceful and even drew the spiritual leadership away from the general population. The result was the use of "war paint." This practice made the members special and lifted them above the rest of the community. This was a time of abuse of spirituality and resulted in a community out of balance.

The sixth clan consisted of the spiritual people of the tribe and was called the Bird Clan. Of course, all Elders were given respect as spiritual advisors. This position of respect was a blessing and was an anticipated time in life. The Medicine people of the Bird Clan were often not elected or selected, but were in this position because they were already in the hearts of the people. Ministering to the spiritual as well as the physical needs of the people required a great deal of intuition, wisdom, knowledge of life's journeys, vision of the future, knowledge of prophecies and a rainbow of abilities to communicate only that which the listener needed and was ready to hear. Cooperation with the natural, knowledge of ceremonies, herbs and songs took a full life-time to learn and perfect. Some nations such as the Dineh and Ojibwa have a group of singers for ceremonies. The head of the Bird Clan is the eagle.

The seventh clan that the Creator put in this community system is the Deer Clan. There are those who say that it was the moose and not the deer who was the leader of this clan. Others in the north claim that is was the caribou who was the clan head. The Deer Clan holds a most intriguing position on the Peace Shield. The position or blanket of the Deer Clan lies in the second circle of the Peace Shield. This is a place of transition as the Human family evolves near to the Great Mystery.

The people of the Deer Clan were known as the "gentle" people. No harsh words ever came from them. They might be called very passive, not wanting to create an energy of separation or conflict. They only wished to weave a web of connection. They desired to make a pathway between life forms. Many were the poets of the tribe, speaking loving and connecting words that attempted to make sense of confusion and bring order to chaos. With this simple outlook on life, they seemed to easily blend in with the natural.

It is said that some of the people of the Deer Clan allowed themselves, at a later time, to marry within the same clan. This violated a natural law. The clan was sent a warning. Their children began to be born with defects and abnormalities, but they still made no correction in their ways. As a result, the Creator removed all of the Deer Clan from this system of community.

It is hoped that those who know the traditions will be able to learn from this event. What other lessons are to be learned beyond the obvious? I believe that this meaningful clan and its teachings will once again be returned to its deserved place. What once was will be

144

again. That which was a great contribution and a very needed aspect of the existence of life will be restored. When we consider the teachings of the second circle - Seventh Fire, I believe there will be more insight.

After the clan system was given to the people, the seven sacred council members sent the seven spiritual beings to Earth. They were to clarify the usefulness of the clan system. These beings came to the people out of the water. The first six beings brought many teachings to the people, but the seventh being came with a blindfold over his eyes. When asked why he came in such a manner and what his teachings were, he replied, "What I have to give, you may not be ready for!" The people insisted on seeing the seventh being uncover his eyes. When he lifted the blindfold from his face, there were screams from the people. Those who looked into his eyes fell over dead. The being went back into the water shouting to the people that he would return when and if the proper time arrived.

While the clan system was in power, the Anishinabe suffered no famine, sickness nor epidemic, no wars and very little violence.

The Teachings of the Sacred Element: Tobacco

In the direction of the east are the lessons and understandings of the sacred element of all Native cultures: tobacco. This subject is one that calls for much "stretching" for most people. This is because of the addictive and harmful effects of chemically treated

145

tobacco on our health. The importance of tobacco is interspersed into the fibers of American Indian culture and philosophy. Examples of the important use of tobacco have already been mentioned in this text:

1. Tobacco was offered to honor an Elder who changed worlds on the Chippewa Reservation.
2. In the story of Baby Boy, a tobacco pouch was left near the cradle board, Chapter Two.
3. In Chapter Four it was taught that children should be taught to offer tobacco with prayers of "thank you."
4. Wildman taught to "place tobacco" when honoring the natural places of Mother Earth.
5. Tobacco was placed inside of the first Water Drum.
6. Tobacco offerings were made to request or receive the teachings of each of the four directions.
7. Tobacco can be placed each day as a "thank you."
8. Tobacco was burned in the Peace Shield Pipe before the sacred bundle of the Peace Shield was opened and during the writing of this book.

Let me say at this point that in my teaching experiences east of the Mississippi River, I have been very surprised by the frequency of the question, "Didn't the Indians smoke marijuana in their Peace Pipes?" Two fallacies exist here. Some people have been lead by early writings whose purpose was to reflect badly on the Indian people by saying that they used marijuana. Because of many barriers between cultures, the Native people were reluctant to explain their

146

practices.

The second fallacy is the use of the term "Peace Pipe" for every prayer pipe used by Native people. This is very inaccurate, and there needs to be more understanding of this issue. Those pipes used in so-called treaty-making councils were probably Council Pipes. They were used for prayers asking for good deliberations and decisions in the council. There are various types of prayer pipes used in Native Culture such as: personal prayer pipe, family pipe, the wedding pipe, the clan pipe, war pipes, changing world pipes, ceremonial pipes and even social pipes. Not yet included in this book are the various lessons and teachings of the Sacred Pipe. Usually those who are known as Pipe Carriers or People's Pipe Caretakers do the teachings which are specific to each Nation's spiritual philosophy.

It has been my direction by those Elders who taught me that the taking up of a Prayer Pipe is a very serious matter. One must have opportunity and apprenticeship for knowledge and training. This truly honors all ancient ones who have spent 30 - 40 years of preparation for carrying a people's pipe or ceremonial pipe or those who do ceremonies using a prayer pipe. I recommend that all who wish to follow this path find an Elder to sponsor them and that time is taken to bring this important instrument into your spirit walk. If you are impatient or do this in haste, the Elders say, "It will back-fire on you and do exactly the opposite."

Briefly, a mixture of non-hallucinate elements were used by some tribes called Kinnikinnik. It is the dried inner bark of the Red Alder or the Red Dogwood and also a small portion of some root such as Sweet Ann Root. If tobacco was available, it was ceremonially added. Due to the unavailability of tobacco on the plains, Kinnikinnik was used. In some Native communities today, only the inner bark of the Red Willow is used.

Now, sacred tobacco is offered for your understanding of further teachings. It is believed that within human beings (Natural People) there is a natural inclination for the presence of peace. One might call this oneness or love for all life or just experiencing a calmness within. For Native people there is the need to experience the nearness of the Great Mystery or to sense the natural reflections of the Creator in nature. It is a special experience to share the Sacred Breath of life and that essence of the breath of the Creator. When in the Sacred Sweat Lodge Ceremony, water is placed upon the hot stones. This allows the visible breath of the stones to purify the participants. As the Native person sees the living Creator in all things, it is only a short step to honor the common element that all Earthly creations use: air and the living breath.

Along with the need to feel near the Creator is the need to touch the sacred. A walk in the woods provides this chance to personally touch and symbolically represents the spiritual presence of the Great Mystery. Many spiritual circles use sacred objects that have a special meaning to the believers.

148

Without going into great explanation here, the planting, growing of the sacred tobacco and the placing of the sacred tobacco in the Prayer Pipe bowl are significant rituals. The lighting of tobacco causes the sharing of the sacred breath of life, another ritual. The receiving of the sacred connects with the sacred in each participant, and the offering of prayers with the Sacred Prayer Pipe are more rituals. A ritual is the result of the teachings of the Elders, the honoring of tradition, the respect paid to Native ways of prayer in order to strengthen the spiritual journey. Each time I do ceremony, I honor my teachers by keeping my promises to them. They have told me, "When you do ceremony, tell the participants what is happening, let them know what you are doing, teach them about these natural ways."

I wish to simply list some of the teachings or uses of sacred tobacco. Those who wish further understanding will seek it out.

1. Tobacco possesses the attributes of both maleness and femaleness. This is an excellent element to lead humankind toward balancing society's male-dominant tendency.
2. In the old system, the only way a pipe carrier could have tobacco for ceremony was to receive tobacco from community members requesting their services. Traditional people expect no other payment for performing ceremony.
3. Tobacco is used with the prayer for the taking of

149

willows for building the Sweat Lodge.

4. Native people make a string of small bundles of tobacco called "prayer ties" which hold their prayers and is similar to a rosary.

5. When making a request for ceremony, one is to pray first with tobacco and then offer it to the Elder. If the ceremony was inappropriate to be granted, the tobacco was either refused or returned to the requester.

6. In many of the Sioux Sweat Lodges, a woman is asked to represent White Buffalo Calf Woman. She sprinkles tobacco around the firepit, making a path from the firepit to the lodge, thus declaring it open for ceremony.

7. The Anishinabe tradition has many occasions to honor tobacco in their ceremonies and stories. The proper use of tobacco with prayer is stressed in the story of The Eagle and The Pipe. The eagle flies each morning to see if there are still prayers being said to hold back the Great Destruction.

8. In the Seventh Fire Prophecy, as we will see later in the chapter, the New People will emerge to retrace their steps to find what was left by the trail. The prophets told them to be careful in how they approached the Elders . . . perhaps some respect and knowledge of tobacco will help them to properly do so.

These are but a few teachings or traditions of the uses of tobacco in the Native Culture. At the present time, there is a mixed message concerning the sacredness of tobacco and the misuse of tobacco. Perhaps the honoring of the true purpose of all things will soon return. Perhaps we will again know that "all is related to all", and each life form has a pure (energy) purpose which is to be respected. We must live in harmony with each life form, giving each the dignity given by the Great Mystery from the beginning of time.

Before leaving this direction of the eagle and the spiritual clan seats, let's consider these brief teachings that lie in the East. The easterly wind is often slow moving, lazy and disagreeable. During my first Sun Dance, the East wind brought a storm that dramatically changed the 110 degree temperature to a chilling 40 degrees with blowing rain. Of course, the ceremony continued at the same pace as before. The most pleasant, easy going, hot day or experience can change drastically to a very spiritually threatening one with winds and storms that can disrupt one's sacred ceremony of life.

In some old ceremonies, the Sacred Pipe was never passed by the east door and never crossed over the east doorway. For some years I directed a program called "The Gathering of Eagles" which brought many Elders together. I learned much and I made some mistakes along the way. But, generally, most Elders knew that my mistakes were results of "not knowing" rather than from "forgetting" what had been taught. One of the lessons that came often was about the Life Line, the eastern path. In most gatherings, the Elder would

151

be able to read the natural signs of the out of doors. My memory reminds me of when a Blackfoot Elder was asked to pray at Arrowhead Stadium at the beginning of the Kansas City Chiefs vs. the Denver Broncos football game. My teachings were to always be as helpful and hospitable as possible, so I followed the Elder around, making sure that all plans were carried out. I joined the group of the Native people on the 50 yard line of the astro-turf. It was a very cloudy day. The stadium was not built along the four directions. The Elder caused a great delay "in the world of T.V. broadcasting and precision timing" that day. He knew that before he could lift tobacco upward and offer his prayer in Blackfoot, he must face the direction of the rising sun or East. It was not important to him to be in front of cameras or the microphone. It took a few long moments for him to ask and find out the eastern direction. Then the microphones had to be relocated after he had already begun his prayer.

Once while I was getting extra chairs for people to sit and listen to the Elders, I was completely oblivious to the gentle Navaho Elder at the front trying to get my attention. I missed his hands motions and facial expressions. Finally, he politely told his apprentice to come to me and have me remove the chairs and people sitting on and covering the eastern path. The Gathering of Eagles was too important and too spiritual to have any obstacles blocking the Spirit Path of enlightenment and blessing.

In this and other such experiences, I truly believe that respect must be given to the symbolic life line/Spirit Path. The traditional

152

people fully honor sacred pathways of illumination, knowledge, healing etc. because, like the first pathway of physical nourishment (the umbilical cord), it is natural to honor the spiritual cord to the Great Mystery at all times. Old Native pottery and basket weavers would be sure to provide a path for the spirit to come and go within a design. They would never obstruct the spirit in any way.

In my construction of the Sacred Sweat Lodge, special attention is paid to honoring the life line. This is just as important as water is to the life line for Mother Earth. Navaho/Dineh hogans face the rising sun, and prayers are offered with corn meal at sunrise. In the Native American Church, tipi lodges are carefully and precisely set up with the door to the exact direction of the rising sun. In some ancient villages, the direction of the center or the Spirit Fire is to honor the desired connection with the sacred life line to the Creator. It has been shared with me that the proper arrangement of a Four Direction Sweat Lodge ceremonial area consists of the central Spirit Fire place. It takes a year marking the sunrise solstices. I understand that the Apache also had a Four Direction Sweat Lodge ceremonial grounds as did the Anishinabe. Such an area was set up near Klamath Falls, Oregon, where I did my first Sweat Lodge ceremony in the early 1980's. I have not seen one since.

A simple Native prayer reminds us of the beauty and lessons of the East Direction:

"We look to the East, the power of the rising sun,

153

where the Elk Nations resides - Black Elk and Elk Nation Woman are. From you (East) come wisdom and understanding . . . You are the power of the Red Dawn and home of the Morning Star. We call on you to bring new knowledge and understanding among the peoples so that all our relations may live. You brought to us the sacred pipe (White Buffalo Calf Pipe) and the Seven Holy Rites. Today we again need the power of the Sacred Pipe to show us the sacred path. The power of Peace lies with you, that can open a flower, send strong roots beneath us, cradle us in gentle assurance of the Great Mystery's love for us. Illumination comes from you to shed light upon our 'journey's path,' help us to see in the night time, to understand that which confuses us . . . . we burn sacred tobacco as we look through the color of the rising sun, the yellow and gold, we have the power to awaken spiritual vision, growth and healing . . . Oh, the day break star that holds the power to awaken us. With each gift from you comes the obligation to use it for the good of 'all our relations!' As we gaze into your sunrise, as a new day begins, assist us to carry out our plans, our resolves, to pray for new beginnings, even birthing new journeys and new questions . . . so that your beauty will bless our every step."

"Thank you, 'Yakoke Abena,' to the door keepers of the East. You have brought knowledge and understanding to the people so that All Our Relations may live . . . ."

Looking to the South:
Rabbit and the Prophecy of the Seven Fires

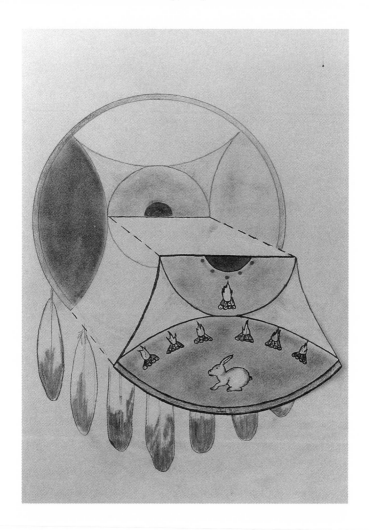

Throughout this book there have been many references to the Seven Fire Prophecy. When the seven prophets came out from the water, their expressions and prophecies were to become the anchors and roots that gave the people an enduring spirit and a will to survive. Now would be a good time to review the three purposes for prophecy in the Introduction as well as the reasons for the Creator to cause a visionary and prophetic spirit.

The color of the south in the Peace Shield is green which represents our homeland, Mother Earth and the place where our lessons are learned. These lessons can be viewed as difficult and painful, or as enlightening to our pathways, thereby blessings us with the fires and guidance of the Creator every step of the way. This direction represents the "hot" and intense time of the day, the time when stress and tension are more prevalent. This is when we have the chance to live out our convictions and beliefs. It is like the third round of the Sweat Lodge, the fourth day of the Sun Dance or the last hours of the Vision Quest or Healing ceremony when we resolve to "Walk with the Creator."

In the Peace Shield, the rabbit is drawn in the South. The rabbit really symbolizes any small animal that is a ground animal. We can sense the softness and tenderness of the rabbit and often associate innocence and trust with this animal. Today these traits are greatly affected by abuse of many kinds, so much so that to trust is dangerous and to be innocent is to be associated with ignorance and stupidity. The Peace Shield teaches that we must develop again the kind of trust that allows us to be tossed up into the air as a baby and have the total assurance that life is a safe and enjoyable place to live. Can we recognize the innocence in each one of us? Until we return totally to the side of the Creator, we are all learning. I am sure that we would alter our behaviors if we were fully educated/experienced in all of life's journeys.

Love and compassion lie in the southern side of the Shield. The rabbit offers us an example of these qualities of life. Many volumes have been written about the current heart condition some may call mental illness of the human race. This heart side of the Peace Shield, as opposed to the head/mind side which lies in the North, really suffers with the heat of day as well as the rising temperature of emotions such as passion, self-doubt, self-love, anger, temper, jealousy, envy, revenge, guilt, etc. It is no wonder that we have tendencies to "go underground" or escape from the heat. We become oblivious to the enlightenment that lies just above our reality. Once we are hidden, we can become tempted with addictions and self-protective behaviors which continue to keep us in darkness. This use of many escape routes only delays our quest for spiritual happiness. One of the greatest losses to the individual is the loss of opportunity to reflect the Creator's love and compassion to the waiting creation that lies above in the "light of day." It is through the understanding and acquisition of the gifts of the North that courage and faith of the South are developed and strengthened.

One rabbit-like aspect in all of us is our defined and often small territory within which we call "home." Home is physical, emotional and spiritual. It is where we choose to live most of our lives. To some home lies beyond this reality. It is a place that we can sense through prayer and meditation, a place of beauty and at-oneness with all life, a place we remember! Our Elders are blessed with some of these places of real home.

In some traditions the spirit path to the Great Mystery begins in the South and travels a northerly direction. A person born in the South, so to speak, must learn to manage their intense emotions of the heart, have the courage to venture out, to go beyond safe zones and territories, to risk more than softness of compassion, and enjoy the openness and freedom that visions and dreams afford.

Some of the failures or limitations of the rabbit are timidness and the inability to see very far. Though the rabbit is very responsible to those near him, he is fearful of what lies beyond his "close to the ground" vision. This can result in unsureness of self because everything seems to be dwarfing him. Everything seems to be so much bigger and more powerful than he. Therefore, he stays within his self-set limits. He has a kind of near sightedness and has great difficulty seeing beyond his own territory. This often causes over-dependence upon others.

Sometimes the mouse is also a teacher of the south. Like the rabbit the mouse perceives everything through its nearness to Mother Earth. He knows the world by touch and smell; the senses can assist him to understand the vastness of the world. A sixth sense, the sense of intuition, is to be developed here in the south.

South: Seven Fire Prophecy

I want to make special mention of a member of the Ojibwa Nation, Fire Clan, Lac Courte Orvilles Band; Edward Benton-Banai. Edward has made available many traditional teachings of the Ojibwa Nation through his writings. He has made many contributions on behalf of his Elders which should be recognized and honored. I have included many of his teachings in the Peace Shield. Benton-Banai's account of the Seven Fire Prophecy, recounted in *The Mishomis Book: The Voice of the Ojibwa*, is the most precise that I have found. Other Elders have provided me with pieces, but it is Benton-Banai's writings that I use most often when presenting this portion of the Peace Shield. Whenever I read this account, I hear Irv Romans, the Peace Chief's voice and spirit once again. His words touch my very center. Irv called them the Seven Great Predictions or Prophecies. They were given to the Anishinabe by seven prophets long ago when the people were peaceful and happy. Each of these prophecies was called a Fire, a period of time during which certain events were to happen in the future of the Anishinabe People. Each Fire is honored in the southern position of the Peace Shield. The Seventh Fire, the time in which we now live, is set within the larger circle near the center.

Some of what the First Fire Prophet told includes:

1. The people must move or they would be destroyed.
2. The people who would decide to move would be guided by the sacred shell of the Midiwiwin Lodge: the sacred Megis shell.
3. The traditional ways of the Midiwiwin Lodge (Elders) would be the source of much strength.
4. The people would finally come to a "chosen ground" at the end of their journey, where food grows on the water. The people should look for a "turtle shaped island" that is linked to the purification of the Earth.

As we journey through these significant Fires/Prophecies, I believe that they have relevance not only to the migration of the Anishinabe Nation, but also great understanding to our own personal earthly journey as well. During the migration, there was a group of men who were in charge of keeping the Sacred Fire. This flame was not to be allowed to die. All campfires were to be lit from this Sacred Fire. At the head of the migration, the water drum and the Sacred Pipe were carried.

Take a few moments now to reflect on our own feelings when we are required to move from where we are. What if we had to leave all that we knew and all of our comforts because something would take our life or our spirit if we stayed? The Anishinabe Nation had become so numerous that even if one climbed the highest mountain and looked in all directions, one could not see the end of the Nation. In our time, we may often feel that life is so full of things, events, meetings, work, etc., that we cannot see beyond all of it.

Having decided to make the move, some means of guidance would lead us to connect with the divine plan. We take "the sacred" with us for the strength to find the place of personal purification which we need in our life. This "sacred" would include the physical as well as the eternal flame that is within each one of us, a flame that cannot ever be allowed to go out and whose coals can ignite other fires.

Within the Anishinabe migration, some who supported the prophecies did not want to move. One group remained behind at the eastern door to care for the eastern fire of the people. Elders today say that almost all of those who stayed behind were destroyed or absorbed by the light-skinned race at the coming of the Fourth Fire. Having looked at this brief account of the teaching of the First Fire, challenge yourself to draw other parallels.

The second prophet told the people that: 1) The Nation would be camped by a large body of water; 2) The direction of the Sacred Shell would be lost, and the spiritual lodge would be diminished in strength; 3) That a boy would be born to show the way back to the traditional ways and that he would show the "stepping stones" to the future of the Anishinabe people.

162

One of the major stopping places during the migration was at "the place of the Thunder Waters," which is known today as Niagara Falls. When the people stopped here, the Megis shells rose up out of the water and greeted them. The sacred fire was then moved to this location and remained there for some time.

The Sacred Shell appeared again to reassure the people of their journey near the mouth of Lake Huron where it appeared to the people out of the water. There are accounts that indicate that the length of time of the Second Fire was quite long. Some groups drifted off to look for a place to cross the great water. There were many births and deaths among the people. Villages and gardens were established. Many neglected the spiritual side of life and wandered from the teachings of the Midiwiwin Lodge because they were preoccupied more with physical survival. Many did not use the Spirit Ceremony and the Sweat Lodge. Yet the Elders kept the Sacred Fire alive. A boy did dream of stones that lead across the water, and the people followed that dream into the lighting of the Third Fire philosophy.

The third prophet told the people that: 1) The Anishinabe would find a path to their chosen ground; 2) They must move their families to the land in the West where food grew on water. On the largest island in the chain of stepping stones, the Sacred Megis appeared again and the people gathered together. The Mediwiwin Way grew, and the clan system flourished on this island known today as the Manitoulin Island, the capital of the Ojibwa Nation. The voice of the water drum was heard again, powerful ceremonies were held, food and game were plentiful.

A group later travelled a northerly route around Lake Superior and settled on the West side of what is today called Spirit Island. The Sacred Shell rose up to the people from the <u>sands</u> of its shore. Some of those who travelled the southerly path also met at Spirit Island, and it was near that place that the words of the prophets were fulfilled. Here wild rice, the food that grows on water, was found.

The Elders of the Midiwiwin Lodge sensed and knew that their long journey was near an end. But, what about the First Fire prophecy of " a turtle shaped island" that awaited the people at the end of their journey? The southern group had seen an island such as this. All of the people went to this island and placed tobacco on its shore. The Sacred Shell rose up out of the water and told the people that this was the place they had been searching for. The Sacred Fire was then carried to that place known today as Madeline Island.

Here, I would like to emphasize a common theme that seems to appear and reappear in spiritual histories around the world. The Choctaw Nation, more properly called the "Okla," followed a sacred pointer having traveled by water from the west. Some have referred to this pointer as the "Leaning Pole." In some accounts, they landed somewhere in Central America. The Elders placed the Sacred Pole in the center of camp each night, and in the morning, it pointed the route the people should take. The pole first pointed to a northerly route and then later to an easterly route across Southwest U.S. to the banks of a great river. The Okla people thought that surely the Sacred Pole would not lead them to cross this large, raging river. Their faith was to be put to the test as they awoke to their Leaning Pole pointing to the east. There was much turmoil among the people, but they finally built sturdy rafts and crossed the mighty "Misha Sapokni" or "Ancient Waters." Some days later, the Sacred Pole stood straight, in the land later to be known as the state of Mississippi.

The reader would not find it difficult to locate many other "pointers" within spiritual circles such as the Bethleham Star, or a pillar of cloud by day and a pillar of fire by night (Exodus), to mention a few. The Pte People went up a spiral cavern from their underground dwelling as they were beckoned by the wolf. For Native people, the pointers or signs that direct their lives were very welcome sights to behold. In our walk of life, we must look for ways that the Creator uses to get our attention.

The absence of signs can leave us guideless and even lead us to think that the Creator has somehow forgotten us. Just as the Anishinabe were given the sign of the deafening noise of the falls (Niagara Falls), so we are given signs that rise up as the noise of life becomes overwhelming. We must watch for them, listen for them and look for them, even in our dream time. Significant "Sacred Shells" will rise up when we need reassurance of the Creator's love and watchful care for us.

Our spiritual lodge does diminish when our journey is rutted and seemingly unbeneficial. When there is so much negativity, violence, depression, apathy and self centeredness around us, it is no wonder that we forget those spiritual experiences that have been so life-giving. We think that our strength will not hold up to the many negative forces and energies zapping our precious life-force. Yet, there can be the emergence of a youthful, childlike spirit that swells up within each one of us which redirects our focus. To many, and to me, it has been the Elders who have planted a vision which enables us to walk more upright, to carry the heritage baton forward to the next "Spirit Island" reality. The "food that grows on the water" will be that which will spiritually nurture us in a place that we could not have imagined. Only because of the "pointers", this book being one of them, have we joined first with the Elders' teachings and then embraced the Spirit Fire within our sacredness. Original teaching and the fire within enable us to stay on course, using our enduring faith as the stepping stones toward the chosen land.

Before hearing from the fourth prophet, I want to look more deeply into those sightings of Sacred Shells. If one was to look more "imaginatively" at the shape of the megis shells, one might notice the remarkable similarity between their shape and that of a UFO. The Native people could be comparing what was sighted to that which was familiar to them.

The evidence or presence of the "above beings", "Star People", little people and flying objects was very accepted by most

North and South American Native Peoples. If any group is ready to include other beings into the phrase "all our relations", it is the Native and aborigine who know their heritage. I believe that those who embrace this symbolism of the Peace Shield and let its spirit energy embody them will also begin to prepare for yet another important journey: a pathway to the stars! Remember the seventh being who appeared to the Anishinabe with a blindfold over his face. The people were not ready to receive his gifts or the sight of him. Thus ends my "seed planting" of new ideas.

The Fourth Fire was originally given to the people by two prophets. These two came as one and told the people of the coming of the Light-skinned race. One prophet told them: 1) The future would be determined by what face the Light-Skinned race wore. If they wore a face of brotherhood, then there would come a time of wonderful change for generations to come. They would bring great knowledge that could be combined with that of the Native people to create a mighty nation. 2) Then two other nations would combine with that mighty nation and create the greatest nation of all. 3) The people would be able to tell if the Light-Skinned race came in brotherhood if they came with empty hands, carrying no weapons. If they came with only knowledge and a handshake, then all this could come to pass. 4) The second prophet warned the people to beware of the new visitors if they came wearing the face of death. The face of brotherhood and the face of death look very much alike. 5) The prophet told the people to beware if they came bearing weapons and said that if they came in suffering, they can fool you.

Their hearts might be filled with greed for the riches of the land. 6) If they are indeed your brothers, let them prove it. Do not accept them in total trust. 7) You will know that the face they wear is that of death if the rivers run with poison and fish become unfit to eat.

It is not my intent to create any more animosity for a particular race of people. I have made previous expressions of our need, as Native people, to honor the past, know the prophecies and participate in the fulfillment of the Seventh Fire. I ask Native and Native-hearted people to look at who they speak with now, to see beyond the institutions they represent or their ignorance of Native history and culture. Let's journey into the bright future that is affected by our prayers and faith.

I remind the other members of the Human family, especially those of the Light-Skinned race, to be joyous walkers with us upon the stepping stones that lay ahead for all Earth people. We are not to be burdened unnecessarily by that which history does or does not record. See the beauty all around us and the job ahead of us to reconcile the results of past decisions and actions. We can all be co-creators again as our biological mother who carried, nurtured and birthed us. Let us dream a vision which can become a reality for ourselves and the generations to follow. Much dialog can be generated about the history of the Fourth Fire. I believe that there occurred a mixed bag of blessings and also "hard to swallow" medicine for all nations and individuals.

Reflections on the Fourth, Fifth and Sixth Fire must be viewed with great awe. It was such a wonder for ancient people to be given these prophetic glimpses into the future. These futuristic glances gave reason to continue the struggle and to endure until the time of the present Seventh Fire. Meaningful contemplation can provide us with more insight into human behavior and reasons for Native behaviors in the heat of possible tribal and even human annihilation. A very real possibility exists to the Humankind today for the destruction of Mother Earth by the "boat people" (again).

Certainly for most Native communities, it was natural to be receptive and hospitable to neighbors visiting their areas. It was also natural to be very generous with food and supplies. The land was abundant with gifts to share with all. Many early visitors to Native culture gave accounts of the cleanliness, orderliness, respect and generosity of the Indian communities. Of course, the prophets of some Indian groups alerted their people to be aware, watchful and slow to trust the actions of their white neighbors. The Peace Shield directed the people to adopt a wait-and-see mode and let the Light-Skinned ones prove their true face. For the Light-Skinned ones, however, the philosophy was more "no time to wait." Progress to the Indian meant slow deliberation while remaining natural and staying true to the nature that the creator provided. On the other hand, progress to the White race meant fulfilling the expectations of those who sponsored you, finding refuge for your belief system, getting the land cleared and civilized, building and organizing a nation.

169

The fifth prophet told the people: 1) There would come a time of great struggle for all Native people. 2) Near the end of the Fifth Fire, there would come among the people one who would hold promise of great joy and salvation. 3) If the people accepted this promise of a new way and abandoned the old teachings, then the struggle of the fifth fire would continue for many generations. 4) The promise would prove to be a false one, and all those who accepted it would cause the <u>near</u> destruction of the people.

Without consulting American history books, much less the reliable memories of oral tradition, we know of the "great struggles" of American Indian people during the Fifth Fire. The Manifest Destiny and intentional legislative actions to "remove and civilize the savages" pushed tribes and nations away from tribal coherence into occupation of unwanted territories with different and often limited resources. Much Native community turmoil and discord were caused by the motivation of spiritual denomination and military personnel to keep this progress going. Much of the leadership was, I believe, personally and politically motivated as well. The disregard for the foundations of Native life, the Elders, the youth, and the land finally led many to focus on basic struggle: the preservation of life and the necessary adjustment to new places and environments.

The "one(s)" who came with a great promise of joy and salvation were clearly different people from different nations. However, their messages of this "new way" were described as the better way for the people who seemed too simple, without religion,

170

or a concept of progress. Whatever the promises, treaties or supplies offered, Native people probably viewed them as a "giveaway" which was not to be refused. The buying and selling of land was certainly a foreign idea.

The abandonment of their "heathen" ways was both the desire of the visitors as well as the calculated outcome of treaty agreements. For captured Native people, one option negotiated was to be moved to a new location or even live with another tribe. To adjust to new living conditions was to abandon one's own walk of life or traditions. This wave of visitors into Native communities gave few, if any, other options. The outcome was the acceptance of "survival plans" for many who did not fully realize the expected abandonment of their life-style and culture. The new way placed many American Indians into a lengthy period of adjustment, struggle and amalgamation upon their beloved land - Turtle Island.

Without placing blame on either side of history, in hindsight, it is my opinion that the promise of great joy was a false one as was predicted. Those who accepted the promise should not be faulted either. Let's look at the cracks in the building blocks of the Native belief system as we review the Sixth Fire.

The prophet of the Sixth Fire said that the promise of the Fifth Fire was false because:

>   1. Children were taken away from the presence and teachings of their Elders.

2. The people lost their reason for living, their purpose in life.
3. A new sickness would come among the people, and the balance of many people would be disturbed.
4. The cup of life would almost be spilled. The cup of life would almost become the cup of grief.

When these predictions were made, many people scoffed at the prophets for some of the following reasons:
1. How could the destiny of the Indian people be in the hands of another nation of people?
2. Could there really ever be a time when the "rivers would run with poison and the fish become unfit to eat?"
3. Children taken away? Never!
Not respecting our Elders? Never!
4. New sicknesses? There were natural medicines to keep all sickness away. Native people were healthy and happy.

New sickness in the form of alcohol, introduced to Native communities, did upset the balance of life. Although they were known for their self-control and discipline during pain and battle, their spiritual and emotional fibers became worn and ragged. The forced round-up of Indian children to live in boarding schools, away

172

from their Elders and traditions, created more separation between the natural life and the invented life. Their own language and religion were taken from the children, and even their appearance was changed by the forced cutting of their hair. The result of all this for Native communities was that the people began dying at an early age. They had lost their will to live.

Fortunately, the prophecies and visions of the Sixth Fire prophet helped prepare the people for events of the future and told them: 1) The ways of the Midiwiwin Lodge would become in danger of being destroyed. 2) All of the sacred bundles were to be gathered and hidden out of sight. Sacred ceremonies were recorded on scrolls and also hidden; So were the teachings of the Elders and the sacred teaching shields. All were to be put under the ground to the safe keeping of Mother Earth. 3) The interpretations of these materials were to be withdrawn and not spoken of again.

As the Peace Chief said, "In the Sixth Fire, the Indian religion went under ground." For the Anishinabe, a time would come when the people could again practice their religion without fear. A small boy would dream where the sacred bundles were hidden. He would lead the people to that place.

In my travels, I have been told of many Native ceremonies that continued throughout the Sixth Fire. There were great restrictions on learning the teachings of the Elders. I believe that much spirituality was embodied in Native stories and legends; also

173

during the Sixth Fire there were recorded inaccuracies and that Christian doctrine was planted or even adopted within Native folklore.

To Native peoples, the adoption of spiritual truths could be expected. The acceptance of truths as well as medicinal treatments, if in harmony with one's belief and vision, were to become a part of one's life. Consequently, the Sixth Fire was a "destroyer" of Native freedom of worship and prayer for all nations. But, for those who knew their prophecies, it was only a "season," a circle which would run its course, a fire to be endured so that it could light the next set of prophecies and ignite the Seventh Fire.

Now, the Seventh Fire prophet looked different from the other prophets. He was young and had a strange light in his eyes. He said that: 1) In the time of the Seventh Fire, a New People would emerge; 2) The people would retrace their steps to find what was left by the trail; 3) Their steps would take them to the Elders whom they would ask to guide them on their journey; 4) But, many of the Elders would have fallen asleep and would have nothing to offer when they awakened; 5) Other Elders would remain silent out of fear or because no one would ask anything of them; 6) The New People would have to be careful in how they approached the Elders. I have always taken groceries; a gift and a bag of tobacco, especially if my visit was for a length of time; 7) The tasks of the New People would not be easy. But if they would remain strong in their quest, the water drum would again sound its voice, the Anishinabe Nation would be

174

reborn, and the Sacred Fire would again be lit.

The Seventh Fire prophecy went on to say that: 8) At this time, the Light-Skinned race would be given a choice between two roads. If they chose the correct road, then the Seventh Fire would light the Eighth and final fire. This Fire would be an eternal Fire of peace, love, brotherhood and sisterhood. If the Light-Skinned race made the wrong choice, then the destruction that they brought with them to this country would return and cause much suffering and death to all the Earth's people. Edward Benton-Benai says that "traditional Mide people of the Ojibwa and other Indian nations have interpreted the two roads that face the Light-Skinned people as the road to technology and the road to spiritualism."

The retracing of steps to find that which was left is happening now. There will be more later concerning the nature and makeup of the New People. Their journey to the Elders, I believe, represents both the spiritual teachings preserved by them and the physical Elders who are living now in the time of the Seventh Fire. It is beautiful to see our Elders, even the Elders within our young people, awaken from their forced sleep to live again in the world. Their awakening is to be honored for they can now speak honorable prayers for the heritage that is in their blood lines. Native people and others must respect their path.

It is the awakening that leads me to seek more from the Elders. Now there is more for all to learn and understand if one

175

chooses to do so. Those who are awakened are also the non-Native as well. They are to be more open to the original truths being brought out for the last time. Grandpa Foolscrow has spoken of the white people who are in the midst of native circles, ceremonies and teachings. He told his people, the Oglala Sioux:

> When those (White people) whose
> ancestors took the ways from us return
> to teach them (traditions), then the
> (Native) people must remember it is
> our Elders returning to teach us!

Some of my first exposure to Native spirituality did, in fact, come from well-intentioned, good hearted, non-Indian young people. These people were among those the Hopi prophesied would go to sit with the Elders.

One might wonder about those Elders in the Seventh Fire who choose to remain silent out of fear and wonder about their reasons for doing so. Perhaps the silence resulted from some form of community shame, tribal position that would censure them or even some denominational influence. It is truly sad to think that our Elders would have such beauty to share but no one would take the time to find them or approach them in a respectful way. Our approach with our Elders must reflect our respect and love for them even if they are among those not allowed to carry forth much of their heritage.

176

The task of the New People to restore Native dignity and heritage will not be easy. Their road will be rocky and lengthy. The mission to blaze trails for the fulfillment of the dreams and prayers of our Ancient Ones requires one to "walk their talk and talk their walk." The Seventh Fire is a time to place as many of the original truths of the Turtle Island people within reach of the rest of the Human Family. In so doing, our brothers and sisters of all races will have the original teachings to apply to their decisions of the future. The time for choosing the best pathways to bring us ever nearer to the Great Mystery and into the next journey is ever before us - now.

The South is the place where healing and balance can take place. A Cherokee brother from North Carolina shared with me some about healing. He was born with the marking on his hand that identified him as a healer. The focus must be on the "cause", and much time must be spent talking to the person asking for help. The person must understand and have a familiarity with the cultural trappings since the sickness is "passed through" the culture to be treated. These two things are most important in the healing ceremony: connecting with the cause and utilizing the culture to "empower" the medicine or healing. It is not surprising that there is a great need for healing energies to reside in the South since it is the most difficult place of the medicine wheel to learn our lessons. Our medicine people know the importance of being in harmony with the natural order of things and to respect how and where healing ceremonies are to take place.

Perhaps it should be here that I insert some things that have been shared with me about the society of healers: the Mediwiwan. I will share only that which has been told to small public groups. Others who desire to do so may fill in the voids. There are eight levels of the Mediwiwin Society. The first four levels are for general counseling. The four upper levels are considered those of specialists. Each has specialized knowledge of healing for certain parts of the body. Some heal with sound, some share knowledge to help people heal themselves. They know that sickness is more than physical. The specialists are very difficult to approach as there is a "buffer" system of people in between the applicants and those from the upper levels of the healing society.

Teaching of the Sacred Element: Cedar

My very first lesson about cedar came from a gentle Omaha Elder who holds a sacred staff. His journey in the later part of the Sixth Fire was to have one foot proudly within his Omaha heritage and the other foot firmly placed on a church (Jesus) path. It was his account of a story of the Native American Church with a divine messenger that helped to bridge the two cultures so that he and his ancestors could live in both worlds. Grandfather Clifton Springer wore his Native prayer shawl when he ventured into Christian circles, prayed with the cedar placed upon hot coals. "Cedar to us means something 'everlasting.' The cedar tree is green in all four seasons of the year. Cedar reminds us of what is everlasting and green all year around."

178

When I do ceremonies now, I teach about the gifts and lessons that the sacred cedar reminds us of. Often the following story is told. It comes from the book, *Black Elk, The Sacred Ways of a Lakota, The Teachings of Wallace Black Elk*, and I include it now in the Peace Shield.

> We are Earth People because we live close to our mother, the Earth. At first we spoke the same language and the same mind. At the end of seven generations, we had a big family reunion and we spoke many different languages. Then everybody went off again. They went in all directions. At the end of that seven generations, we had a family reunion and we spoke even more languages. Each time our people came together they had to understand that we are a part of the fire and a part of the rock, or Earth, and a part of the water and a part of the green, or living. In that way we were able to communicate with all the living beings. And so, we spoke many different languages, but we still spoke the same mind. So we know where we came from. We still know our roots.

The color green is painted in the South of the Peace Shield. Green represents the living Mother Earth, the home place of us as human beings, the innocence of the heart. The seven sacred beings in the Anishinabe tradition instructed the boy to tell the people about

179

the first Sweat Lodge. They said that the women should prepare the grounds of the Sweat Lodge for the ceremony. Their final act would be to gather cedar for the ceremony. The women would sprinkle the cedar over the alter and down the life line coming from the eastern door of the lodge. Then the ceremony could begin with the lighting of the Sacred Fire.

I honor the teachings that every Sacred Sweat Lodge ceremony for which I pour water must include the balance of both men and women. Even for a Men's Lodge, the women and young girls will prepare the cedar with laughter and pleasantness. Then, before the Sacred Fire is lit, the area is cleaned and the cedar is taken into the area by the females in a proper way.

Flat leaf cedar is usually preferred in most ceremonies and is used continuously throughout the Sun Dance Ceremony from beginning to end. Perhaps it is the gift of cedar to move energies out from a sacred space that makes it so important in such ceremonies. I do not feel comfortable with describing this as "removing evil spirits" because this gives more credit to negative forces. All energies must be respected and may even be requested to leave a space when asked. Cedar is often used in house blessing ceremonies to "move out all energies" before the sacredness is honored and the sacred space is restored.

The early American pioneer families used to throw cedar into fireplaces occasionally to give the house a pleasant odor and feeling.

Little did they realize that cedar waits, as do the other elements, to be given the opportunity to help humans with their special giftedness given by the Great Mystery.

The lessons of the South are used to help a person find their true path or purpose in life. It is for the reconnection or reestablishment of our relationship with Mother Earth. This includes what she produces, what we learn from her while we are here with her and the lessons of growth that we learn in her presence. The southern winds that bless new growth also teach us to have "friendly winds" with the creation and with those we meet. The Elders also say that the wind from the South is an industrious spirit/energy, to get things done which open doors to growth and change, to do so before the hotter season of summer. The power of the South is the ceremonial time, the time for the Sun Dance. The mineral of the South is the precious "pipestone," the petrified blood of the Elders mixed with the soil of our Mother Earth.

A prayer is given now to remind us of the lessons and beauty of the South direction.

Aho! We look to the South, the place of the most difficult lessons of life to live and learn. We give our thank you to the Spirit of Prophecy that prepares our earthly journeys, provided us with the trust, guidance, and courage to survive life's journey with hope and joy. To the power of the South we pray for healing

181

and abundance, that the warm sun may bring forth the Flowering Tree. Assist us with your power of the Hoop, the Sacred Hoop of all the peoples, to lead us to harmony and balance as we dance together in the sacred circle of peace. Around the sacred tree of green may all peoples gather and grow; grow in our trust in each other and in the natural laws of the Universe. We pray for the time to "go out into the world," for the testing of our ideas and methods, pray for the fulfillment of our vision and wisdom to be given to the world. It is through the gifts of cedar that we honor lessons of eternity and everlasting love of you, the Great Mystery . . . We place sacred tobacco upon our beloved Mother Earth.

"Aho Thank you" - "Yakoke Abena" to the door keepers of the South. You have brought us the gift of prophecy and the lessons of the rabbit. Continue to remind us of the love of Mother Earth and all she provides for us. We welcome the lessons of growth and change, innocence and trust, so that our " every step is a prayer" upon our beloved Mother Earth.

Looking to the West: The Bear and the
Seven Sacred Megis Shells/Spiritual Journeys

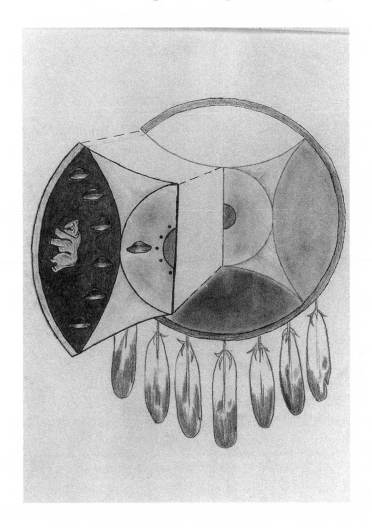

With enlightment and truth we honor the birthing power of the West, the gifts of the bear to internalize truth and the many spiritual journeys led by the Sacred Megis Shells.

The concept of power is so falsely represented in today's society. When I was young, power was something outside myself that would seem to increase my power. A Roy Rogers cowboy cap gun on my hip, a wooden sword and especially a hand-made bean flipper gave me, I thought, more power. Later, my twin brother and I made Indian bows and arrows that made our power to move "from us" to a target. Looking at our children now, we still see even more power sources outside themselves. Occasionally, some mention is made of inner personal power in areas such as the martial arts.

Later, in my youth, I did find power in my athletic ability. This too, however, gave a rather superficial image of power that obviously dwindled in my later years. In my early adult years, my mind and social years made a living for me and my family as a counselor/teacher and mental health family therapist. These years were often founded upon "outside myself" ventures and happenings and later, unfortunately, I realized that I hardly ever revealed the real person inside. Being that eagle person, I viewed life around me riding the winds of other people's traumas, personal tragedies, needs, etc. I gave myself little time for taking personal inventory and returning closer to the side of the Creator. I lived my life as others would want me to or as the community dictated. Consequently, my power was really their power directed toward and at me. Motivation was still initiated by sources outside me. What appeared to me as power was really energy begun within others, within organizations, etc., that had not been passed by the "West side" of me. The sacred side or holy part of my creation is honored in the "look within place" on the sacred Medicine Wheel. I can now say that the coming of my personal vision and the Sacred Peace Shield being placed with me greatly coincides with the landing, hibernation and birthing of Rainbow Eagle. As another creation seeking the presence of the Great Mystery, I can speak much more honestly with myself.

The Sun Dance Chief who sponsored my prayers and steps in the Sacred Mystery Circle for four years, Grandfather Jim Dubray, often said: "These four things you must do and tell others to do."
1) Respect yourself
2) Organize yourself
3) Discipline yourself
4) Humble yourself

Also, you "must turn a negative into a positive. Dok-Sha!"

Resting for awhile in the West side, I realized that often I had prayed for everyone else, for all the Universe and now I needed to finally pray for myself.

Aho! Looking to the West one finds the beauty lessons of the "look within place." Here one takes honest inventory of one's strengths, fears and weaknesses. In one walk around the Peace Shield, the eagle intentionally grounds himself, sees the realities up close as the rabbit and must settle once again into the womb of the West for self nurturing and love. Sleeping was never a problem for me until the spirit path awoke within me and forced me to more honestly respect the lessons and truth of the West. "Going into oneself" was, for me, contemplation and thinking, even preparing for a task to be done with forethought. Now I hear the Elder speak, "Find joy in the silence. To achieve happiness you must know yourself. To know yourself is to heal yourself."

A story is told about a village of people where there lived an old Medicine Man and a younger Medicine Man. As the younger Medicine Man learned more and more, he watched for his chance to out-do and eventually become the village's Medicine Man. Being impatient, he devised a plan to trick the old one so that he could step up into the "honored seat."

His plan was to capture a little bird, cup the bird in both hands, walk up to the old one and ask, "Be this bird dead or alive?" If the old Medicine Man said that it was alive, then the young one would squeeze it to death and open his hands. If the old one said that it was dead, the young man would open his hands to reveal the bird alive. This would all be done in the presence of all the village, and then the young Medicine Man would have proven his power over the old one.

One day the village gathered around. The young one chose this moment and walked up to the Elder one saying in a loud voice,

"Be this little bird that I hold in my hands alive or dead?" The gentle one looked over the villagers and then into the eyes of the young man. Finally, he said, "It is entirely up to you!"

Aho. The journey to find oneself, to learn to know oneself and to work out one's joy and happiness, is entirely up to the individual. The West is the birthing or rebirthing place in one's life. It is the honoring place of our human birth, the womb and the placenta that nourished us, the honoring of motherhood and Mother Earth. Often, the Pipe Ceremony begins with the recognition of the spirits and gifts of the West.

Native American Church ceremonies are conducted in the West of their tipi lodge, and it was within this void that the Great Mystery fulfilled the great vision. From the West we look across the Medicine Wheel or Peace Shield, gather the power of the Creator from the center and receive the gifts and lessons of the East. This gives balance to our lessons of the West. The Vision Quest, the spiritual birthing of one who fasts and prays, is given place in the West with the power of the bear who goes "within" to find the resources necessary for survival.

On one of my Vision Quests, I was blessed with hundreds of butterflies. While meditating I heard them flying. I thought that birds were flying by my face. An old story is told from Lakota memory:

At a time long ago, a camp was in chaos, and the people were is disharmony. A butterfly came and sat on a woman's shoulder. He whispered in her ear what was to be done to help the people and bring harmony to the camp.

Many times in my counseling I would come to a condition of "no answers" for troubling issues. Then this butterfly spirit would inevitably find its way to my spiritual ears and tell me of answers to try.

The Vision Quest is a valuable gift from the Great Mystery. Remember the baby - now old man who visited the council of elders and brought back gifts, including the Vision Quest? To others he brought the capability to seek out the knowledge of the Spirit World through fasting, dreaming and meditation. We must believe that answers to our questions in life are within the void, womb, dream lodge. The Elders teach us that our goals, visions and dreams lie in the West. To carry them out depends upon our strength and art of interpretation and meditation.

I give my respect to a sister of mine that I've yet to meet, Brooke Medicine Eagle. She has great beauty of truth for both men and women to understand. In her book, *Buffalo Woman Comes Singing*, an excellent resource of ancient wisdom, especially regarding the womb, void, the "Moon time," she speaks of this time as "the time when the veil between us and the Great Mystery is

188

thinned , . . a time . . . of calling for vision . . . Native Grandmothers teach us that this time is never used for ourselves alone; it is always used to pray for 'all our relations.' "

Women use moon time to call vision in the moon lodge, to bring vision and to receive teachings in the dark of the moon to give to community in the full phase of the moon. I believe that many women today are looking back on the old trails toward the ancient teachings in an attempt to reclaim and honor their feminine aspect. Later, I will refer to some teachings of the Sacred Pipe and the sign of White Buffalo Calf, "Miracle," that challenges both men and women to honor and respect each other's male and female energies.

The West wind is noisy and boisterous, creating most of our weather patterns. In the West is the home of the thunderbeings who gives us much needed rain to restore the Earth Mother after drought. The power of the West restores "the way" and gives new life as water runs through the veins of Mother Earth. The thunder beings are always terrifying and sometimes test you to check your resolve. They remind us of the source of both the power to bring life and the power to destroy life.

The color black is located in the West on the Peace Shield. The Peace Chief said that "the light (yellow/sun) of the East will penetrate the darkness (black/night) of the West." To the Plains Indians, black represented a lifetime dedication to the Creator. It represented the Spirit World, so the color black carries meaningful

189

significance. The darkness (the womb) has been a place of growth and development. It is a place of creation in the void, a condition of new beginnings to be given the light of day, a place of rebirth.

The Bear: Medicine - Seeker of Truth/Honey

The bear has a variety of lessons for humans to contemplate. We will cover only a few of the many helpful anecdotes about the bear symbol on the Peace Shield. One interesting story comes from the Anishinabe tradition which tells of the bear's coming to the "surface world." Many beings, including the bear, at one time in the distant past had humanoid forms and lived below the surface of the Earth. The bear and others were chosen by the below-the-surface council to somehow assist the humans. Bear helped the humans by pushing up the first Tree of Life (the cedar tree). Afterwards, he followed the others to the surface. His inquisitive nature led him to take a look at the pitiful humans. After seeing many humans, bear understood why they needed help. "They didn't even have claws, or fangs, or much fur at all!" Because bear established the Tree of Life as a channel of communication between the world above and the world below, Native people believed that bear should be given proper respect.

Bear also deserved much respect because he acts as guardian of the many secrets which help cure diseases. Remember that the Bear Clan was known for their knowledge of plants that could cure the ailments of the people. In the Sioux tradition, there were Bear

190

Dreamers who discovered healing herbs in their dreams and brought them to the people. The Anishinabe anticipate the Northern Lights (Aurora Borealis) each year to "come out to dance when the Bear Power is in its highest strength." And in the Seneca tradition, the Bear teaches brotherly love.

In the Peace Shield teachings, the strength of the bear/bear person is the ability to search, to seek the honey of truth. This need to find all of the honey, or truth, is very strong. Sometimes, the need can exceed judgement which can cause rushing into other territories or trampling small growth. Bears are amazingly fast for short sprints, and bear people tend to rehash the same issues over and over again. If they are not very playful, Bear People might need to consider that their light-hearted natures need to be increased.

Bear power is reborn in the spring when they come out of their dens. There is a great tendency in bear people, however, to remain in their dens just a little longer. Companions of bear people must be prepared to be patient until their partners are fully ready to meet the spring. Often, the introspection time in the den births new ideas and projects that must be acted upon and nurtured to their adult form. It is said that some of the failures of bear people stem from their self-doubt. They must take time to hibernate, they can be unforgiving in protecting their territory and will act apprehensively at times.

191

The Seven Megis Shells in the West

Across from the West lie the lessons of the clan system that greatly assisted community to function efficiently and effectively. The gifts of the clans provided the cement that would build strong foundations and government. Here in the West the focus is more upon the effects of spirituality, prophecy and "travel pains" upon the individual and family, rather than the community at large. Each appearance of the sacred shell pointed to individual decisions that needed to be contemplated.

Let us recall the six times that the Sacred Megis Shell appeared to the Anishinabe people as they left their beloved homeland in the far Northeast. I ask the reader to more fully meditate and apply these spiritual journeys to one's own life experiences. The first time, the sacred shell led them away from their homeland, a place where they had been living a full and peaceful life. The nation was very large and powerful with a system of overland trails, more than ample food from land and sea. Many people did not want to move. One group that did not move was called "The Daybreak People." Most who stayed behind were destroyed or absorbed into the Light-Skinned people at the beginning of the Fourth Fire.

If we were among those who had to decide whether or not to leave our homeland, the decision would be very difficult. We would be leaving a very comfortable and balanced life. The prophecies told the people that they would be destroyed if they did not move.

Perhaps we have found ourselves in similar circumstances. Often it is more difficult to follow Spirit than to remain in familiar and comfortable conditions. I am sure that many did not want to believe the prophecies, but went along anyway to "follow the crowd." The fascination of following a sacred shell added more incentive, especially when very mysterious prophets came out of the water to warn and help the people.

The <u>second</u> time the megis shell rose up out of the water and greeted the people was at the place of the Thunder Water. This was certainly a positive sign to the people that confirmed their decision to leave their homeland. One can imagine the thrill and joy that each person felt and the community shared.

The <u>third</u> time the megis shell again appeared to the people out of the water. As we track the journeys of the people, we can see that the trip was already taking its toll on the emotional health of the people. Attacks from nearby nations kept them insecure. Finally, they camped by a body of fresh water, and then the sacred fire rested for a long time. Accounts tell us that at this time, there were groups that drifted off from the main community. This splintering caused the choosing of loyalties. Strong voices pulled the community apart.

The <u>fourth</u> appearance of the sacred shell occurred when most of the nation traveled North and settled on Manitoulin Island. This was another reassurance of their journey. Food was plentiful and powerful ceremonies were held.

193

The nation now had split into two groups; one travelled a northerly route and the other a southerly route. They eventually met at a place known today as Spirit Island. Here, the fifth appearance, the Sacred Megis Shell "rose up to the people from the sands of its shore." A reunion of the two groups surely brought optimism and joyous feelings as they once had at the Thunder Waters. An additional sign of hope appeared when the people found the prophesied food that grows on water. This renewed their faith in prophecy.

The sixth appearance of the Megis Shell on the people's journey occurred on the "turtle shaped island" that is today called Madeline Island. Their sacred pointer spoke to them that they had finally reached their destination. The main body of the Anishinabe people gathered here and became strong and powerful. Some say that it took 500 years to complete the journey, and the Sacred Fire was kept alive throughout that time.

The incomplete story here lies in the prophecy of the First Fire Prophet who stated that the "turtle-shaped island will be linked to the purification of the Earth!" Perhaps this has more to do with the bringing forth of truths that will lead to the purification of the world. In my travels, I have become more aware of gifts and teachings of the Seventh Fire than ever before. This tradition seems to be a modern day pointer to the promising and hopeful future. The Peace Shield attests to the fact that there will be another journey to make by a larger group than just one or two nations.

I believe that the <u>seventh</u> appearance of the Sacred Megis Shell is yet to come. The Sacred Shell will appear once again to reassure us, the Spiritual Walkers, of the next journey and yet another big family reunion. What kind of "thing" would rise up out of the water, speak to the people and have the mobility of a flying machine? Take a second look at the Megis Shell. Could it resemble the shape of a UFO?

The seven Megis Shells in the Peace Shield represents the seven times that spirituality has played an important part in Anishinabe life. If we were to travel with them as members of the nation, I believe we would be able to see the parallels of what happened to them with the experiences that face us and our children in our present times. We probably haven't had the blessing of a divine intervention, such as a shining shell, to reassure us of our journey. Perhaps some of us have had such experiences that have helped to realign our course and reassure us of the steps we are taking.

Turtle Island people have received a long-awaited sign of spiritual intervention. On August 20, 1994, on a small buffalo farm in Wisconsin, a white (not albino) calf was born and aptly named "Miracle." It is believed that this has happened to reassure those on a spiritual journey that they are headed in the right direction. There are a number of other reasons that this miracle has happened. Like the sacred Megis shell, Miracle came to remind us of many teachings. Miracle's birth is a sign of the return of the spirit of White

195

Buffalo Calf Woman who brought the Sacred Pipe to the people. This marked the beginning of the Pipe Age and the completion of the Rock, Bow and Fire ages. It is not surprising that this fourth age is signaling us to not only seek spiritual ways, but also to fulfill the Anishinabe Seventh Fire prophecy; to go back on the old trails and pick up what the ancient ones had left for us. We are now given the message to pray by many grandmothers and grandfathers.

Miracle is reminding us of the coming of the Spirit of Unity and the enhancement of spiritual energy to again unify and become balanced. This message is in harmony with the Pipe Age and tells us of the importance of balancing male and female energies within each of us. The gifts of the female energy should be honored in as many institutions as possible. This is also a strong teaching of the Sacred Pipe. The pipe brings together the bowl (female/Mother Earth) and the stem (male/Father Sky) and thus creates a "third existence" in the balance. Native Suzan Hargo said of the sign Miracle, "It is an important sign of well-being and comingness being on the verge of an awakening."

In this direction, the West, we are emphasizing and honoring the personal journey. This is a time that spirituality has played an important role in each one's spiritual quest. Grandfather Hollis Little Creek told me that in the old days, a person only requested the Sweat Lodge Ceremony for themselves seven times in their lifetime. This is done out of respect for the ceremony and the elements involved. The seven appropriate times to request the ceremony are:

196

1) A Blessing Ceremony when a baby is born.
2) A Naming Ceremony.
3) A Rite of Passage/Vision Quest/Puberty Ceremony.
4)The Beginning of a Marriage or Vocation - Acceptance of a request to join one or more of the different socities.
5) A specific purpose/change of vision
6) When one's knowledge is to be left behind.
7) The last Sweat Lodge Ceremony in a lifetime.

In some traditions, soon after the time of changing worlds, the personal Sacred Prayer Pipe is taken to all the places that the person has been to in their life. This might take one to two years to complete. Then a final "spirit releasing" ceremony is held.

Teachings of the Sacred Element: Sage

There are different types of sage. The type that I will be referring to in this section in sometimes called "prairie sage" and has soft leaves. The "white sage" can be used in similar ways, but in these teachings I speak of ceremonial sage. Traditionally, the women are often asked to gather the sage for ceremony. This is not, however, a hard and fast rule. Often there is very little explanation of how the elements function in a ceremony or why they are important. After years of ceremony, I would like to add to my understanding of the sacred element of sage.

Sage is usually placed around the ceremonial or prayer pipe in the Sun Dance. This is because of the significant gift of the element sage. Sage has the ability to "insulate" the sacred within. Although some use sage for protection, it also holds the sacred within a space so that its power will be honored and therefore insulated from those with struggling energies. The protection is, therefore, for the participants and the supporting people rather than for the prayer pipe. When sage is constantly burned in a teaching space or ceremony, the purpose is usually to hold the "helping spirits" in that place.

Ceremonial people make proper requests and invitational songs and prayers to the helping elements of ceremony. Preparation of the sacred space is most important for the visits of the Holy Spirits. Presence of the spirits in a ceremony does not necessarily mean they will choose to help. Special prayers to request such help are given with humility and patience. Sage can be used to preserve the sacred space while waiting for ceremony and the spirits. Sage is also used at the close of a house blessing to seal the sacred and honor the sacred that is already present.

Sage had another gift. It can be thought of as like a "sponge." Sage is a type of "collector of energies" as are certain crystals. Sage collected from a sacred land, such as Bear Butte, South Dakota, carries special energies from that place. Some years ago, at the end of a ceremony, an Elder cautioned some innocent bystanders to not take the sage that surrounded the Sun Dance Circle. He said, "You wouldn't want to take all these prayers and things away from the Mystery Circle into your home!" An intense circle of prayer energy had been established. Thousands and thousands of Prayers of all kinds had been placed in that Sacred Circle with the Sacred Tree. Why remove them? Why risk taking these prayers and energies into your home? Prayers made in the Sun Dance Circle are to remain there for a whole year. The surrounding sage holds the sacred and the prayers and energies, as does the Sacred Tree.

We now offer this prayer to express our thanks for the lessons and beauty of the spirits of the West.

> Aho! We look to the West; the place of the setting sun, that brings the nighttime. The dream lodge is set up to welcome the spirit messages. Here we honor the "go within" place, the womb of our first mother, where we honor our daytime lessons and growth, use the gift of introspection, and we are completely honest with ourselves. Here in the darkness of the West, we let the brightness of the truths of the East illuminate the shadows. It is the West that holds the accumulated knowledge of the Universe. We honor the giftedness of Bear Medicine and the drive within us to seek out the honey of truth. From this home place of the thunderbeings, we welcome the life-giving rains of the storms that often unsettle us. In the West we release that which holds back and

burdens us on our spiritual journeys. Truly knowing ourselves enables the healing process to begin. In the darkness we encircle ourselves with sage to honor our sacredness and give thanks to our Creator for being with us and at our sides at all times. Your strong words will bring us out of our solitude or depression, to go forth, rebirthing our specialness and our visions. Winds of the West, thank you for self-worth. With your rains we nourish and water the beauty within so that we can restore our personal dignity and pride. We look to the setting sun with a smile for the Sacred Shells that appear upon our spirit path and the whisper of the Spirit Helpers to bring light to our shadows of uncertainty. We place sacred tobacco upon our Earth Mother.

Aho! Thank you! Yakoke Abena! Thank you to the door keepers of the West. You have shared the gifts of the bear and the importance of going within, honesty and the taste for truth. You have given us hope and light in the darkness, the spiritual helpers and guidance of the sacred pointers. The Great Creator waits to assure us of the blessings of the spirit journey. It is your lessons that challenge our personal missions and visions. Continue to guide us on the Sacred Red Road into the next rising of the Sacred Megis Shell.

Looking to the North:
The Deer and the Gifts of the Seven Feather Truths

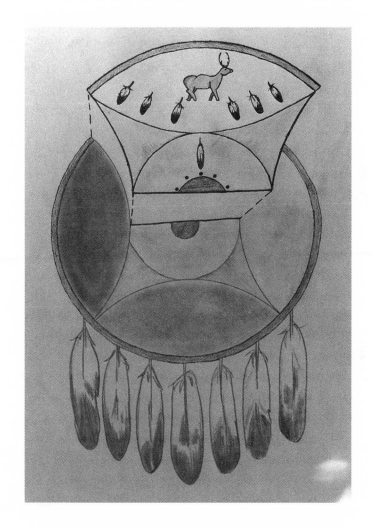

This side of the Peace Shield holds the energy and spirit of the Ancient Ones, the grandmothers and grandfathers and those who are the Elders to come. As I have mentioned, we are now seeing younger Elders who are accepting their roles in prophecy to honor "their Elders" in the return of the Indian Spirit.

Within this lodge of Elders are also some self-appointed teachers and ceremonial leaders, both Native and non-Native. These are often thinking people who can communicate well, but have often buried their heart issues. There are also Elders who speak from lives penetrated with hurt, pain and a variety of other emotions, including hate, revenge and anger. And, there are those who feel ready to share, but who have not had the opportunity to learn their own heritage or Native spirituality.

Some of our Elders are unable to look over large barriers that stand so high that ancient truths and beauty remain distorted, misrepresented and slanted. There are those with whom I have visited in nursing homes who hold on to their beauty and hope. However, they have no community or youth with whom to share or teach. In the midst of this situation, there are those who step out into the masses with humility and wisdom and attempt to paint the colorful murals of ancient pathways. These lessons are just as meaningful and relevant to our present life today. Their motives are pure and in harmony with their vision. They are able to go into any territory with peace, joy and respect for every life form. With humility and dignity they carry their pride as a child would ride a spiritual horse, as elders who knows themselves, have healed inside, who sense their companionship with the Great Mystery.

One of the joys of my travels has been to watch the Elders interact with the young Native people at culture camps. Nothing can compare with the change that comes over a grandmother who sits with a young person and converses with more than her voice. Those tired eyes and hands speak loudly and with such a glow and radiance. Her smiles erase every earned wrinkle in her face, and her unspoken stories shine from within as with a child who has learned to whistle or tell a joke for the first time. Yes, it is in the lodge of the North that our Elders of all kinds and races are housed, our Elders of the past, the present and the future.

In the North lies the winter season that forces us to have some level of respect for the prevailing conditions of nature. Even the youthful and energetic must adjust to the white and cold weather that forces them to consider the "purifying" conditions of winter. For our Elders, this is not a time to challenge nature, but to stay indoors, both physically and spiritually. Many will change worlds during this winter season. Winter is well known for being a purification time for both animals, humans and Mother Earth.

Mother Earth looks forward to this cold season to sleep, dream and to pray that truths will blossom in the spring. Our Mother forces her human children to respect her. We often disregard her water ways, ignore her polluted oxygen/breath and damage her inner passages for breathing and respiration. Upon her breasts lay more and more non-growing materials. Inner toxins are released through pores in her surface. She prays that the coming days of balance between holding one's energy together and the releasing of one's growth pattern will be delayed. She wishes for this delay for the sake of her human children and all life forms who look to her to provide their home.

Winter is an opportune time to bring people together, often outside of ceremony, a time for sharing stories and crafts. I am reminded of my visits with Lakota Grandfather Dubray, who after his teachings and lesson, he would say, "Well, that's it, that's your snack for now!" It is also a time for us to spend in contemplation of life issues and to seek clarity. Clarity of purpose and action at this time can lead us to purity of motive as well. Those who possess such clarity can then be a clear and bright light to others. As the white snows would clean and purify, so would one's actions be cleaned as well. The spirit of creativity is also at its height at this time.

The cold winds of winter are mean and vicious, setting up an energy of endurance and courage. Such testing of one's limits quickly brings repressed memories of the blistering, hot conditions of summer. Such reminds us of the changing and unexpected events, happenings in our lives that are "earthquakes" and "blizzards" for us. Now we don our blankets of memories of those ancient ones who were not given choice in their steps of prophecy. We pull to us that which warms us, body, mind and soul. Sacred Fire is again carried within us to endure with courage the often unmerciful act of Old Man Winter. We prepare our "Giveaway" things for ceremony, friends, family and the Elders who carry our traditions in their hearts.

Purification is overcoming separation (alienation) from others and anchoring to our source, the Creator. Purification is reducing distraction from our lives, yet it is not free from anxiety or fear. Purification is the reduction of the distractions of life, the expressing of emotions and not being overwhelmed by it. The most effective tool of purification is undisturbed prayer and fasting. Then we can anticipate the spirit of renewal and the springtime with Mother Earth with the blessings of our resolve. One's contemplation, honesty, purification and purity of true spirit being a renewal of Greenness. One's life is opened, and one becomes ready once again to "give all" to life.

The Deer: Who Sees Both Near and Far

Here in the North, the drawing of the deer is painted green on the Peace Shield. First, what is the deer trying to teach us? For what purpose is the deer dancing and running by our awareness? Those born in the direction of the deer, or who are conditioned to be affected by the North, are described as "thinking" and "logical" people. Their purpose is to easily disregard the mystical and strengthen the logical and objective points of view. If not balanced with the warmth, compassion, innocence (being able to act without reason or purpose as a child) and the heart aspects of the South, such

205

a rational mind will have what might be called "cold wisdom." Such cold winds of truth are given with very little sensitivity to the situation or the listener.

The color green leads a great Shield Walker, who has many such traits, to nurture and balance the self with the gifts and lessons of the South. If there is no such balance, one will become mind-dominated and unable to give vision of the future and optimism and hope to the community in their Elder years. Often a different purification occurs as no spirit of recovery (renewal) of "forgiveness" is given space in one's life.

Another interesting characteristic of the North presented by our green deer is the ability to see both close and far away AT THE SAME TIME! Few animals can do this. Perhaps this is the reason why deer is the most successful mammal to adapt to all sorts of habitats. Imagine what this would be like for a moment. A similar example that might assist is that the human female has the ability to think and feel, to see and sense from both sides of the brain at the same time! Men are more inclined to utilize only one side of the brain at a time. I am being careful to not imply that one is more gifted than another here.

Most Native traditions, in more ancient times, emphasized and gave importance to the female roles in their societies rather than to the male. One reason that I found in the Anishinabe teachings says the Elder taught that, by the design of the Great Spirit, female beings have primacy over males . . . . All female beings symbolize and embody a portion of the Great Spirit's life-giving force. They are said to be automatic conduits for power from the Spirit World.

Because of seeing so much at one time, the deer is very prone to panic. This is a result of seeing more than they are able to understand or seeing too much for their level of security. This can create a world of panic, fear of what cannot be explained or just narrow-mindedness that limits the capacity for spiritual growth, imagination and mystery. In fact, the mule deer (no pun intended) never follows the same path twice. He is not willing to risk being "found out" by predators who sense his insecurities.

The balanced deer person could take a lesson from our Buddhist neighbors. Buddha is often pictured with a deer. Deer often represents innocence and a return to "the natural." Most critical to deer people is the need to balance their keen intellect, senses and awareness with the tenderness and innocence of the child within. They must make more room for the unknown and mystical and work hard on patience to internalize the unexplained, the "twilight zone."

Briefly around the Peace Shield, difficult lessons lie ahead for the Eagle who must respect the inner self, the grounding. The rabbit must think things out to explain the shadows that keep them near home. The bear must learn not to rush through other's territories in his search for honey, and the deer-minded people must learn to also feel what they know and learn to love the adventure of mystery.

207

I challenge the reader to explore these few examples. The gift of the Peace Shield is to plant seeds that can be watered with insights and truths.

The Seven Great Gifts or Teachings of the Peace Shield

Review the story in chapter two. Out of the vessel came seven great gifts to be given to the people. The council taught the boy that for each gift there was an opposite.

The teacher spirit within me will be more evident in this section of the Peace Shield. In my vision, as shared in chapter eight, I was given the image of many teaching circles being facilitated by a number of Elders. I was told by the oldest Elder's helper that each student would be in a group with other students like them. They would have had the same lessons and experiences in life. Their Elder/Teacher would also be very understanding since their life had been like the students.

In this part of the Peace Shield I will be making allowances for the many levels and experiences of readers who are adding these truths to those already with them. Little teaching prompts will be given with each of the Seven Great Teachings/Gifts. The Elder within us is to be our Elder/Teacher, and the students in our group are to accompany you on this similar journey. It is my prayer that you take a winter time with each gift and use much patience and self-love (forgiveness).

Here are the Seven Gifts of the Sacred People. Each is represented as a Eagle Feather in the North of the Peace Shield:

1) **Wisdom** - to cherish knowledge is to know wisdom!
2) **Love** - to know love is to know peace.
3) **Respect** - to honor all of the Creation is to have respect.
4) **Courage/Bravery** - Bravery is to face the foe with integrity.
5) **Honesty** - Honesty in facing a situation is to be brave.
6) **Humility** - Humility is to know yourself as a Sacred part of the Creation.
7) **Truth** - Truth is to know all of these things.

These lessons/gifts each have an opposite that must be understood just as clearly as its counterpart. Each gift has a twin that reflects the essence of itself. Native Spirituality teaches to see all of life as meaningful and important. The hard lessons, or shadows, are equally significant as the colors and beauty we see in the sunlight.

In the spirit of our ancient ones, the grandfathers and grandmothers and the Elders yet to come, I place this homework upon you. In the spirit and energy of the White Buffalo Calf Woman, who came out of the North, the white buffalo who is the great provider of all the needs of the people, I grant my blessings upon you. With each gift, there are a number of water nourishing opposites that must be known and discussed. Use the purifying season in spirit and in the physical to soar above and see the beauty of the world, honor one's innocence, have compassion and love, nourish one's thirst for truths and burn sweetgrass so that the prayers of the elders can accompany your journey.

Teachings of the Sacred Element: Sweetgrass

As our council of Elders are forever connected to Mother Earth, we too are so closely related to her that her gravity holds us to her surface as a loving mother holds her dear children. The teachings of the Sacred Sweetgrass call to us to respect the Great Life Form that is within and around Mother Earth, as well as the ancient ones who remain "at one" with her.

My first lesson of the sweetgrass was told to me by an O-da-wa (Ottawa) Elder, Angus Pontiac, in the Province of Ontario, Canada. His life was filled with much struggle, yet in his elder years he was among those elders with whom I travelled across the U.S. one summer. Each evening, at sunset, he never failed to take the Eagle Feather off his cowboy hat, light sweetgrass and quietly pray. He taught me that a long time ago, the elders observed that the animals would not eat of a certain tall plant in the fields. So, after prayer and meditation, the Creator told them that this tall, green plant was to be

210

used by Indian people for a special purpose in their ceremonies. First, it was to be gathered by the elders, then braided as one's hair to honor Mother Earth. This would represent our dependency and love for her. Our Elders say, sweetgrass is "the hair of Mother Earth."

Second, the fragrance sent by the sweetgrass will notify the ancient ones, the council of elders in the North, that "sacredness" is honored. This fragrance invites spiritual grandparents into our sacred space.

Third, the burning of sweetgrass reminds us of its "total giveaway" to our spirit path. As I have taught, the beauty of life, "a changing of worlds, " is actually happening before our very eyes. Let us honor its journey.

Some traditions teach that sweetgrass was the first plant to grow on Mother Earth. To place its fragrance and smoke on us is to represent our desire to be near the wisdom of the Old Ones. I once travelled with a Blackfoot Elder, Gerald Melting Tallow, as we journeyed from Calgary, Alberta Canada to the Navaho Reservation. I noticed that before he could get on the airplane, he lit sweetgrass "so that the grandfathers and grandmothers could all gather his spirit to go with him." None of his spirit would be left at home, to ensure that all his spirit would travel with him. His gift to each tribal elder that he met was sweetgrass. In his broken English, he would explain its use. To my knowledge, this was the first gift of sweetgrass to the Navaho area by a Medicine person. It was included in some of their

211

ceremonies and is still sought by some ceremonial people today. Sweetgrass was not a native plant in their area, but was more prevalent in the Northern USA and Canada.

There Are Other Teachings

There are other lessons and memories of sweetgrass, but this will be sufficient for now. When there are enough interested students of the Peace Shield and Native Spirituality, there will be seminars and workshops to use these teachings in therapy, healing circles, community organization, educational and rehabilitation programs and personal spiritual journeys. Also, the Peace Shield has an even greater purpose - to gather, nurture, birth and develop world peace and harmony.

In the North, the Spirit Keepers and Faith Keepers are waiting to reveal further wisdom as we are prepared to receive it. Other sacred bundles such as the Peace Shield bundle are to be opened and interpreted to their Nation first, then to the rest of the human family next. Will humankind have a void, a space into which these life-giving truths can come to? Are the various spiritual circles ready to be respectful enough to come into the Great Lodge of the Creator?

Now we offer this prayer saying thank you for the lessons and gifts of the spirits of the North.

Aho! We look to the North, the place of our wisdom.

To the ancient ones who continually pray for us and who stir within us our spirit of eldership, we say thank you. We thank the season of the winds of purification, the energy of endurance and courage to purify our resolve and motives. We send the fragrance of the sacred sweetgrass as we desire your presence, wisdom and guidance in our ceremonies.

We hold tightly to its braids as we caress our Mother Earth in the changes that are a part of her growth. In our prayers to the Great Mystery, the Spirit World that lies in the North of the Medicine Wheel, we ask for your assistance to learn the Peace Shield, to use its power of truth to balance our mind and hearts and steps back to the side of the Creator. It is renewal we seek, it is sweetness of truth that we seek, it is compassion, trust and faith that we seek. It is spiritual freedom in the sky of the four directions we seek. For the lessons of the Deer and the Sacred gifts from the Elders Council, we look both far and near with eyes of faith and understanding. We lift sacred tobacco to all our relations of the Universe and place it upon Earth Mother.

Aho! Thank you! Yakoke Abena! Thank you to the Door Keepers of the North. We have learned of the lessons of the Deer and the Sacred Gifts from the Sacred Council. Thank you for your

213

prayers that stir the Sacred Mission within our eldership.

These words I speak as a Seventh Fire Peace Shield Teacher to those who want to honor these teachings. Your study and inclusion of these Peace Shield Teachings do not make you a Peace Shield Teacher. One must not only be in harmony with the physical symbols and their power, but also in oneness with the Spirit of the Peace Shield. An apprenticeship to a Peace Shield Teacher and then a ceremony to honor one's commitment to appropriately teach the basic truths are necessary. Then "the rest of the story" of the Peace Shield will follow. Supervision by one's elder/Peace Shield Teacher will guide the teaching of seminars and workshops which should be done together.

Knowledge of the Sacred Pipe Ceremony is required since the Peace Shield has a Prayer Pipe bundle with it. Respectful display of the Peace Shield is also required in a place of honor. But, it is the spirit of the Peace Shield and the Teacher who bring it into total awareness!

A STEP INTO THE FUTURE - JOURNEY TOWARDS THE LIGHT/SPIRITUAL LODGE OF THE CREATOR

The year is 2023. Journey with me to the local library on Second Street. Let's go to the archives where the old newspapers are systematically stored, newspapers from New York, Washington D.C., Chicago, St. Louis, Kansas City, Oklahoma City, Denver, Albuquerque and . . . well, let's just say the West Coast. My steps are slower now. My age is that of the Elders I knew back in 1996, such as Grandmother Twylah Nitsch, Mother Theresa, Roy Rogers, Nelson Mandela, the Dalai Lama, Grandfather and Grandmother Ross.

I have contacted the procurer of the archives for help in retrieving a few major news articles involving American Indians since the turn of the century. Yes, I told the group with me, it was old news, but also very interesting. In fact, it was mind boggling to think that only a few decades ago those people of the Earth viewed life in such limiting and narrow ways. There have been so many great changes in our vision of the Earth, her relationship to us Earthlings, her relationship to the entire solar system and our relationship to the Universe. Much purification has taken place and, hence, much enlightenment, stability and spirituality.

Here we are, sitting around an antique oak table, looking at each other with such pleasant smiles and radiance. The news clippings before us reveal the impact of these changes upon the people of one culture, our Native Ancestors. With one glance, we say thank you once again to those who, with faith and courage, opened our vision to our spiritual potential.

The names of the journals, the selected reporters and editors, places and dates of events have little to do with the "revelations" that took place back in those days. Now, as we reflect on such "unveilings," they seem rather minimal. It is strange to think that those in the late 20th century could be so unimaginative and unaware. Those times were monitored by "many" because humankind was so close to completely annihilating all life upon Mother Earth. Many were indoctrinated with a variety of forms of fear. It seemed that violence and fear producing tactics were everywhere. We can certainly count our blessings today as we have finally achieved a form of peace and harmony with ourselves and our "extended family." Our gratitude goes out to many who caught our spiritual attention so that we would step into the future with joy, hope and optimism, having ignited our sacred flame within. We wish to honor those known as Wisdom Keepers, Elders and Ancient Ones.

With no regard for order or sequence, let's survey these articles again. It is something like holding blank pages before a book is written, an empty canvas void of an image of color and form or a newborn baby born to live through a fantasy that has become real. Through the written manuscript we can experience vicariously what each reporter experienced. And we were here to first read about it, to actually see and . . . . Here are portions of the lengthy news copy:

HEADLINE: "Native Americans and Others Reveal Their Belief in Flying Saucers!"

This reporter was first contacted two weeks ago to interview three Native American Wisdom Keepers from both North and South America. The voice on the phone said they were ready "to openly reveal their belief in and encounters with flying saucers." That I was selected to personally witness Native and Extraterrestrial beings in council from afar was both amazing and an honor. Clearly, this story took precedence above all others, and the events that will be reported changed my life forever. The encounter between the indigenous and the "above beings" did occur. This is my story; however, the scope of this story is much more than these words.

While traveling with the two spokespersons of the Elder, I was again told of regular contacts by UFO beings, especially in meeting places in South America. I was told that this had been occurring for centuries. They told me that many journeys of Native Peoples had been guided by objects they called Sacred Megis Shells. These Native emissaries spoke of some traditions that Original Man was lowered to Earth by a space ship. I was told that my personal and professional life had been carefully monitored and that it had been decided that my spiritual nature was conducive to being selected as the first reporter of this significant and PLANNED event.

218

As we approached the chosen site, I wondered what my reaction would be. I was told that "they" could read my thought and would alter any part of my copy if necessary. Then, as if the sun cleared the clouds, I felt calm and peace as I stepped from the room. I was ready! We walked beyond the grove of trees into a clear field. From a vantage point on a hill, I saw the Sacred Medicine Circle where this interplanetary "council" was to occur. Then, from the trees, appeared three Native people who walked into the Sacred Wheel in the East doorway, and then I saw . . . .

Other headlines read:

"E.T.s MEET WITH NATIVE PEOPLE - WITNESSED BY REPORTER"

"E.T.s / INTERPLANETARY CONFERENCE WITH NATIVE HOLY PEOPLE"

"NATIVE PEOPLE HAVE MEETING WITH THEIR SPACE RELATIVES"

We pick up another article and read:

OLD INDIAN SHOWS SUBTERRANEAN PASSAGEWAYS

As a reporter of thirty years, I am to give this first-hand account of verification of existence of communities living within the Earth. Following the exact directions of a letter written to me, I boarded a plane to the Southwest. The writer of the letter said that an old American Indian man was ready to tell about and show the portholes to underground communities.

After landing, I waited for an envoy to meet me. The letter indicated that I had received clearance to be the one to release this information. It also said that the military had been notified of this plan six months earlier. Specific instructions were given so that no interference would occur.

I soon realized that there were four of us charged with reporting this event. The others were also given the same directions and detailed plans to follow. I concluded that we represented four major papers which would report these events to the world.

After being picked up, we were given a sheet of paper that said, "The following three objectives are going to happen:
　　　　1) You will respectfully interview the Native man.

220

2) You will be taken to the passageway and allowed to enter.

3) You will meet four beings. There is to be no interview.

My professional demeanor almost went out the window. The others seemed superficially poised for this once-in-a-lifetime experience. I think that we felt a common bond with humanity for the first time.

The van pulled up in front of a simple, frame house with a stove pipe coming out of the front room window. Through the window, I could see the outline of the old couple as they huddled together and then came to the door. They opened the door and said, "We've been waiting a long time for this to happen. Come on in and listen."

Other headlines read:

"STAR (UFO) ELDERS AMONG INDIANS SINCE 1940's"

"SUBTERRANEAN COMMUNITIES DO EXIST!"

"REPORTERS MEET WITH UNDERGROUND PEOPLE!"

"NATIVE AMERICAN INTRODUCES REPORTERS TO 'UNDER-THE-SURFACE' PEOPLE"

221

A third article read:

NATIVE AMERICAN EXPOSES THE EXISTENCE OF A PLANETARY COUNCIL OF E.T.'s

After writing the first article about my personal invitation to the face-to-face meeting of some Native Elders and Extraterrestrials in New Mexico, I was surprised to answer my front door and see the same two Native spokespersons. Some years had passed, and the level of public reaction had finally subsided. The two did not come in, but said, "You are asked to witness and report on a World/Planetary Council Conference in four weeks. No recording devices, writing materials or satellite surveillance will be permitted. Will you come?" I responded without hesitation, "Yes!" "Then," they continued, "in four days you must first go to see Grandmother." They handed me a paper and left with no other comment. The paper read:

THERE IS TO BE NO PRESS RELEASE OR PRE-CONFERENCE COMMUNIQUÉ OF ANY KIND.

AFTER THE COUNCIL MEETING, A NEWS RELEASE WILL BE GIVEN TO YOU. YOUR NEWS ARTICLE MUST BE WRITTEN BEFORE YOU LEAVE AND WILL BE CORRECTED AND APPROVED. THIS ONLY ARE YOU TO PLACE INTO PRINT.

For some three years now, there had been technically safe travel to and from Sky Stations. Rumors of high-level diplomatic gatherings had been circulated, and the travel was an adventure that I would welcome. But it was the council that jangled my nerves and intrigued my imagination.

My first stop was to visit with another Native American - a Grandmother. After being left there on her walkway, I was greeted at the door by a pleasant, smiling face. She was quick to ask me all kinds of questions as if she were interviewing me. She went straight to the core. "They say that you are honest. Tell me about yourself."

It was later that Grandmother said, "They know that you are the right person for this. You can be trusted to write only what they say you can. They have watched you, and your spiritual condition is almost ready! This is my job . . ."

Grandmother related to me that Native People have known of and honored such a Council of Elders for thousand of years. They have appeared to humans as Native people look, but have other images as well. Looks are not important to them, and they can read minds. Their purpose, since early history, has been to intervene, when necessary, on behalf of the Great Mystery. They were to provide teaching shields so that the Earth people could find harmony and peace with themselves and the Universe. Grandmother also told me of the things I needed to do in order to be prepared for this assignment. After completing these preparations, I should return to

223

her two days before the Council meeting.

For some time, Grandmother taught me how to send my thought telepathically, to feel the messages of vibrations and to see the beauty in all things. She then said, "It's really good to be prepared, but it's not necessary to know about everything. That is where your innocence comes in."

For the next two days, I listened and was instructed by Grandmother. Late on the last day, she said, "Now I have a Blue Light Special for you! Remember the special visitor known as the White Buffalo Calf Maiden who brought the Sacred Pipe? Just before she appeared to the scouts, she was brought by a blue light. The ancient ones knew of the many times that the blue light had been around. Sometimes, at night, it floated over those who needed special attention or who were given special "honors."
This story is told by the ancients:

"A young Anishinabe man fell in love with one of the singing girls who came in on a giant clam shell (space ship). It landed and rose with the sound of the maiden's singing. The young man couldn't get close enough to the beautiful maiden, and one had grabbed his heart and, in turn, he loved to grab her. A stag deer came to him, changed into a man dressed in deer-skin, willing to help him. The young man finally captured his "star maiden" with the aide of his helper. I'll tell you the rest of the story when you return. But, know that all around the helper was a radiance of blue light. The helper said to the young man, "Your heart is known to me."

When I left Grandmother, I knew what I had to do to prepare. When I returned, Grandmother told me of the marriage of the two. The young man and the star maiden had a son. But, the star maiden was lonely and her husband built a sky ship of birch bark, and she "sang" herself and her son into space . . . ."

In two days, I was to "go into space" on this assignment! I was ready, thanks to Grandmother. It was on Saturday that I stood before the Space Taxi . . . .

The next headline:

"NATIVE PEOPLE INTRODUCE 'BIGFOOT' AND 'THE LITTLE PEOPLE' TO REPORTERS"

* * * * * * * * * * *

These glimpses into the near future are the result of messages sent to me by some of my spirit helpers. Several Light Beings have been invaluable assets in the production of this book of teachings. They, like angels, have provided considerable light energy to my heart as well as to my writing hand. It has been the gentle, loving spirit of the Great Mystery that has infused these words and illustrations with energy of love and light.

The Peace Shield is ancient, but it is a very real bridge that can and will take us into the future. The truths of many spiritual circles are to become a <u>flowering tree</u> that blossoms and reaches toward the Light. We, also will reach toward the light and the Great Source of Peace. We will walk on pathways toward other islands of spiritual residence, led by what I believe will be the Seventh appearance of "what looks like the Sacred Megis Shell." This will be an identified flying object from our Sky Relatives sent to assure us of yet another spiritual journey. We must decide to take this journey or we will be destroyed. Our journey will lead us to yet another chosen place that is definitely connected to the purification of the Earth and all her inhabitants. We shall continue our journey there where the "food of enlightenment and peace" grows on top of the waters of new awareness and knowledge.

Before we are confronted with the decision to either journey on toward the Spiritual Lodge of the Creator or remain in our present places, we must consider this challenge which is offered to us. How deep are your roots? Are you able to remain upright and stable when the winds of change blow into your life?

Each plant has sufficient rootage to receive nourishment and to dig deep into the soil. This rootage gives such a sense of love and care from the Creator. It is no wonder that, to the trees, it feels so good to spread their roots in all directions as if to say, "Hold me close, Mother Earth. You give me food and comfort. Thank you! Now I can send my upper self to those who are in need of my gifts."

226

From this calm security, the plant gains self-importance and is able to grow. It extends itself upward toward another reality above ground.

Native people know the importance of fully "grounding" oneself with the Earth Mother. Our roots are strengthened by our harmony with the natural order of life. Native tradition has served our medicine people for centuries. Ceremonies were designed to be in complete oneness with the healing energies/forces. All energies and creations are birthed by our Mother. We spread our loving thoughts and prayers through and toward her. The Great Mystery instilled within Earth Mother such potential for all things to "become" and grow toward the upper dimensions of life's evolution.

Now, all humanity must follow suit in the giving of our appreciation and our respect for our Mother. Spiritually and symbolically, unless we send our roots deep within the soils of truth, within the nearness of the Creator as represented in the Peace Shield, the winds and storms of change and purification of the intense rains will, most assuredly, diminish our faith and trust.

Remember the "Seventh Being" who rose from the water with a blindfold over his eyes? The being said, "What I have to give, you may not be ready for!" The being will return if and when the proper times comes. People at that time were not ready, so the being is yet to come, whether in that form or another. Now that we are in the Seventh Fire, that time is truly in our future. When this happens, we will truly understand how the Fish Clan of old felt as if "one foot here and the other in the world to become."

As represented in the Seventh Sacred Shell in the circle near the Creator, the journey before us calls for personal decisions to be made. Will each of us be ready at that time to decide to journey nearer to the Creator? Will our roots be deep and strong enough to handle whatever lies before us? May the Seventh Feather of truth assist us to hear the message of the Deer Clan and see their demeanor of peace and gentleness. As they use, once again, the beauty of rhythm and rhyme in their poetry, may we too desire "to make pathways between Life Forms!"

Will we be so connected and related to the Universe that when it is time to meet the Great Council of Elders, we will be strong enough? Will we be able to communicate "heart-to-heart" telepathically and not be distracted by appearances or robes unlike our own? And when sacred vessels are placed before our eyes (as in the story of chapter two), will we see things never before seen, realize a tomorrow that is more important than technology, become more than our earthly dreams allow? When we receive their divine gifts that advance us to greater levels of inter-relatedness with the Planetary Family, can our vision include all of this?

As the teachings unfold, *the millennia of perfect peace,* peace with who we are and with each other, is within reach of all of us.

228

The faithful, who will remain to create the Fifth World here on Earth, will be rewarded with new abilities . . . that will be used for the good of all . . . . The idea of learning through opposites will be replaced with a Knowing System that sees all lessons as equal . . . know the joys of becoming the wisdom rather that seeking it outside (ourselves) . . . see through the illusions that were formerly created by pain . . . the connections between all life-forms will be seen, and the Divine (life) Plan set up by the Great Mystery will unfold . .

the Planetary Family (will learn) how all vision is self-fulfilling prophecy . . . (As was before, will come again). The First World was that all life-forms were made of love . . . laughter . . .was contagious . . . instinctive harmonious living was present . . . the balance of peace had taken root and the First World sang the praises of Grandfather Sun's warmth and love . . . the language (of love) was spoken silently with signs and expressions of the face . . .*

*Excerpts from *Other Council Fires Were Here Before Ours.*

It has been my prayerful intent to prepare the young people (the faithful ones) to step into the future with these teachings. It is my hope that this will help us to look ahead to the very interesting and promising pathways ahead and to "the becoming" and the manifestation of our spiritual journey. As we personally live each precious moment of our lives "to its fullest," our dance with All Our Relations will beautifully communicate our unconditional love for all

229

creation everywhere.

In time, our Mother Earth will ultimately "take on a blanket of living light" and become the shining star into which she is evolving. Let us all anticipate and prepare, even celebrate, our journey toward the Spiritual Lodge of the Creator. Such an eventful future! We will return to the state of oneness and harmony within our flame from the Sacred Fire ever before us. Though destined chaos and growing pains will surround us, we must hold onto the joyful warmth of the Spirit flame, follow the enlightened pathway and sing the songs of happiness and peace.

Aho! Yakoke Abena! "All of Creation" (Choctaw Language)

Chapter Eight

STORIES TO BE TOLD WITH THE PEACE SHIELD

STORY ONE

The Great Mystery's Vision

Whenever the young people ask questions, the old ones think about their questions and give their explanations and answers in the form of stories, songs, prayers, rituals and ceremonies.

Gitchie Manitou, The Great Spirit, had a vision. In this vision was seen a vast sky with stars, sun, moon and Earth. Earth was filled with mountains and valleys, islands and lakes, plains and forests. There were also trees and flowers, grasses and vegetables. The Creator saw beings walking and flying, swimming and crawling, and witnessed the birth, growth and end of things.

At the same time, the Creator saw other things live on. Amidst change there was constancy. Songs were heard, as were cries, laughter and stories. The Creator touched wind and rain, felt love and hate, fear and courage, joy and sadness. Gitchie Manitou meditated to understand the vision. With great wisdom, it was most important that his vision had to be fulfilled. The Creator had to bring

231

into existence that which had been seen, heard and felt.

Out of nothing, the Creator made rock, water, fire and wind. Into each one was breathed the breath of life. On each was bestowed a different essence and nature. Each substance had its own power which became its own soul-spirit. From these four substances was created the physical world of sun, stars, moon and earth.

To the sun, the Great Mystery gave the power of light and heat. To the Earth was given growth and healing; to water - purity and renewal; to the wind - music and the breath of life itself.

On Earth, Gitchie Manitou formed mountains, valleys, plains, islands, lakes, bays and rivers. Everything was in its place. Everything was truly beautiful.

Then the Creator made the plant beings. There were four kinds: flowers, grasses, trees and vegetables. To each was given a spirit of life, growth, healing and beauty. Each was placed where it would be the most beneficial and lend to Earth the greatest beauty, harmony and order.

After plants were created, animal beings were brought into existence. Upon each was given special powers and natures. There were two-legged, four-legged, winged ones and swimmers.

Last of all, Gitchie Manitou created human beings. Though

232

last in the order of creation and in the order of dependence and weakest in bodily powers, humans were given a great gift - the power to dream.

The Creator then made the Great Laws of Nature for the well being and harmony of all creatures. The Great Laws governed the place and movement of sun, moon, earth and stars, the power of the wind, water, fire and rock, governed the rhythm and continuity of life, birth, growth and decay. All things lived and worked by these laws.

Gitchie Manitou's Great Vision had now been manifested and brought into existence. *

*Adapted from "Ojibway Heritage" by Basil Johnston.

STORY TWO

Nokomis/Grandmother: A Creation Story
"How Did Our Mother Earth Come Into Being"

As the seasons passed, Original Man and Grandmother lived in harmony with Mother Earth. They picked berries, smoked fish and dried meal all in accordance with the season. They stored much food to get ready for the approaching winter.

In the winter, as they sat in the lodge trying to stay warm, Nokomis told Original Man many stories. He had many questions for her about the mysteries of the Universe, and she answered them the best she could. He asked, "How did the Universe begin?" and "How did our Mother Earth come into being?" Nokomis answered, "Grandson, first there was a void in the Universe. There was nothing to fill the emptiness but a shaker. Gitchie Manitou was the first thought . . . that thought was sent out in every direction. It went on forever. There was nothing on which to bounce them back. The stars you see at night represent the trails of that thought. First, Gitchie Manitou created the Sun so that light would assist the creation. Then the morning star was created. Then, the Creator tried to create a place on which to place life. One attempt turned out to be covered with ice. On the fourth attempt, Earth, as we know her, was created. This was pleasing to the Creator so "singers" in the forms of birds were sent.

The Earth was arranged in the Universe so that Sun and Moon would alternate walking in the sky keeping watch over the Creation. The sun would keep watch during the day and the Moon would keep watch during the night. It is this movement of the Sun and the Moon that we imitate in ceremonies today when we pass things around in one direction.

It is said that when the Earth was young, She had a family. The Moon was called Grandmother and Sun was Called Grandfather. The Creator of this family is called Gitchie Manitou. The Earth is said to be a woman. In this way, it is understood that woman preceded man on the Earth. She is called Mother Earth because from her come all living things. Water is her life blood. It flows through her, nourishes her, purifies and changes her.

On the surface of Mother Earth, all is given four Sacred Directions: North, South, East and West. Each of these directions contributes an important part of the wholeness of the Earth. Each has physical as well as spiritual powers, as do all things.

When she was young, Mother Earth was filled with beauty. The Creator sent singers to carry the seed of life to all the four directions. In this way, life was spread across the Earth. The Creator placed the swimming creatures in the water, gave life to all the plant and insect world and placed the crawling things and the four-legged on the land. All of these parts of life lived in harmony with each other.

Gitchie Manitou then took four parts of Mother Earth and blew into them using a Sacred Shell. From the union of the Four Sacred Elements and the breath of the Creator, man was created. It is said that Gitchie Manitou then lowered man to Earth. Thus, man was the last form of life to be placed on the Earth." *

*Adapted from the source: *THE MISHOMIS BOOK, THE VOICE OF THE OJIBWAY,* By Edward Benton-Banai.

STORY THREE

Rainbow Eagle: MY VISION

PART ONE:

At sunset, near the homeland of my childhood, (Wyandott, Oklahoma), I was requested to lie spread eagle on my back upon Mother Earth. The scenery and culture around me was totally Native American and I knew I was being prepared for a specific ceremony. A middle-aged Native American man was on his knees to my right side, taking two flesh offerings from my left upper arm. He was taking my sacrifice/giveaway to honor my service to "Hashtale"/Creator. In complete trust, I allowed this ceremony as he was following the direction of his Elder. I felt no fear, no pain, knowing of my love for the Great Mystery. There was no indication of shedding blood.

On my left side, near my legs, I soon noticed a familiar face. It was one who has been around for a long time, since my journey on the Red Road began. He wore my power colors!

Now the same Native man spoke to me. "You are to stay physically fit . . ." then, referring to the flesh offerings, he said, "Use this to bless all things, to bless everything." I was then told that I would be told when I should participate in Sacred Sun Dance. This was a complete surprise to me, as I never desired to participate in this very involved and sacred ceremony. However, some years ago I had attended Grandpa Foolscrow's Sun Dance on the Pine Ridge

237

Reservation, South Dakota.

PART TWO:

Next, I was sitting near the front center of a round-like room. Firelight was splashing on everything even though I saw no visible fire. The young man who took my flesh offering now came into the room wearing a buffalo headdress that came to his waist. He passed by me and my helper, not wanting us to recognize him. Then, various Elders spoke to the people and Spirit, letting me know which ones were sincere and those who did not have pure motives.

PART THREE:

A spokesman announced it was time to get ready for the traditional Buffalo Dance Ceremony. I went to the back of the ceremonial area as I usually did when a ceremony was to take place. Soon after I sat down, the Buffalo man began to lead the people in single file into the dance arena. Then, in front of me appeared my Spirit Guide. He was looking rather stern and had a directive expression on his face. He said, "No, you are to no longer sit in the back, you are to sit near the circle where the Buffalo Dance is. You are no longer to remain in the background." I got up to move closer and then he said, "Go dance . . . it will come naturally . . ." I was directed to get in the single file line and dance. Soon, I was to pull out of the line and lead those following me to set in motion a second line of dancers . . . .

PART FOUR:

After the Buffalo Dance was over, the spokesman said, "Each of you is to go to a group (different teaching circles), and the Elder there will understand you completely for he will have lived a life just like yours." Such a calm and peace came over me to think I would be taught by a teacher who would fully understand me and my life. Others in that group would be like me as well. As I walked to my circle, I saw many other groups forming.

I looked into the circular structure, and it was packed with people. There was no room except for the Elder's seat in the West. The Elder's Seat consisted of corn stalks tied together with a back lifting upward off the floor. I walked in seeing a small space just to the left of the Elder's seat.

Then the Elder came to the doorway in the East. His hair was braided in two braids, and he had such a loving, kindly look in his eyes. The way he stood looking at everyone silenced all there. He truly knew and understood each person there. Without hesitation, the Elder spoke, "You (looking at me) place the Elder's seat where you are, and you sit there in it." He turned and disappeared from view.

STORY FOUR

NAPI Gets Angry

The Blackfoot people say that Napi is a lot of things, but he has some unusual characteristics that can be spoken of. He is never satisfied with himself, he looks for trouble, is never kind, and he is always hungry.

One day, he sat himself down beside a lazy mountain stream. He had hunted all day with no success and was hungry, very hot and tired. So, he dangled his feet in the cool water for a time as he sat on the bank. While looking at the water, he thought he saw something on the bottom of the stream bed. He thought it looked big and round. Then the water settled a bit and Napi saw that the object was a "big, red, juicy steak."

He immediately dove into the water and tried to swim all the way to the bottom to retrieve the steak. But, no matter how hard he tried, he couldn't reach the steak. He climbed out on the bank to look at the steak again. There it was on the bottom of the stream bed.

Being creative and very smart, Napi devised a plan. He tied stones onto each of his ankles and wrists and a big stone around his waist. Napi thought that he would sink quickly to the bottom so he could get his steak! In he jumped. He reached the bottom quite easily, of course, and began searching around for his dinner. Being very hungry, he waded as quickly as he could around the bottom, which made the water very muddy.

He was also a bit thoughtless about how long he could hold his breath under the water. Napi suddenly panicked. He wanted to go up, but he couldn't because the rocks were holding him down! In desperation, he remembered his knife on his belt, cut himself free and rose to the top of the water very tired and bewildered.

Laying down on the bank, he went to sleep until his hunger pains woke him. Looking up, Napi saw a tree with its branches bending over the water. At the end of a branch was a bunch of berries that looked a lot like the steak that he saw in the water. Napi sat up. He looked at the water-steak and at the tree berries. He realized that the berries were the steak that he saw, reflected in the water.

Napi began to get very angry, first at himself and then at the tree for bearing berries instead of steaks. He got angrier and angrier. He got so mad that he did something that no one else would ever think to do. Napi took his knife and went to the tree with the berries. He chopped marks up one side of the tree and then marks down the other side. His anger made him do this. To this day, these trees that have berries on their branches hanging out over the water also have cut marks on their trunks. This reminds the Blackfoot people of the anger of Napi and how not to be like Napi and be able to see life all around and always be respectful.

241

STORY FIVE

The Story of When the Snake Had Legs

At the beginning of time, the Great Spirit created all of the animals and creatures and sent them out into the forest. At that time, all of the animals could speak with and understand each other. The Creator was proud of each new creation and watched them with great joy. Yet there was one creation that seemed kind of special. This creature walked on two legs and was also very creative in its thinking. The name for this creature was "Human Being."

A troubling thing was happening, however, with the Great Spirit's Human Beings. Every time one was created and sent out into the forest, it disappeared. Great Spirit was upset about this and decided to call all the animals together for a meeting.

When all were gathered together in a circle, Great Spirit asked who knew what was happening to the Human Beings. All of the animals looked at each other and shook their heads. None knew. Great Spirit then gave them four days to go out into the forest and watch. They were to be alert and find out what was happening to the Human Beings. After four days, they would meet again in the circle and report what they had seen.

All of the animals agreed and left the circle to go out into the forest. One of these animals was the very smallest. You certainly know him and maybe he is one of your favorites: Mosquito. Now, Little mosquito went bussing about in the forest, and he kept his eyes open to find any clues about the Human Beings. As he was flying along, he suddenly saw something ahead in a clearing. "Why, there is one now!", he thought. "There is one of Great Spirit's Human Beings now!" As mosquito watched the Human Being, someone else was also watching. This watcher was snake, and he was thinking, "Aha! Lunch!"

Now, snake looked a bit different back then because then he had four legs. He looked like a big lizard crawling through the grass. As mosquito watched, snake slowly and quietly sneaked up on the Human Being and gobbled him up! Mosquito was shocked! He immediately rushed up to snake and said, "I saw you, snake! I saw what you did! You are the one who has been eating Great Spirit's Human Beings! I'm going to tell!" Well, snake did not like this situation at all, and he said, "Oh no you're not!" Mosquito responded, "Oh yes I am!" And snake answered, "Uh-Uh!" To which mosquito said, Uh-huh!" Now snake knew he had to do something about this determined little mosquito, so he reached up, grabbed mosquito, opened his little tiny mouth and plucked out his little tiny tongue! This not only hurt, but now mosquito could no longer talk. Snake's problem was solved.

Soon the four days of observation were over, and it was time for the animals to again gather in the great circle. The Great Spirit asked, "You have all had time to watch. Who now knows what has

243

been happening to my Human Beings?" All of the animals looked at each other with blank faces. But suddenly these was a buzzing, and mosquito began to fly around the circle of animals. When he came to snake, he hovered over his head and pointed down while buzzing loudly. Great Spirit asked, "Mosquito, do you know something?" Mosquito began buzzing even more loudly. Now, Great Spirit can understand all of his creatures no matter what language or sounds they use. He knew what mosquito was trying to say. He looked to snake and asked, "Snake, do you know what has been happening to my Human Beings?" Snake immediately shook his head and said, "Me? No, no."

Now, Great Spirit is very wise and knows when we speak the truth and when we are lying. Some of this gift has been given to all parents. The Creator knew that snake was not speaking the truth. After thinking for a few moments, Great Spirit said, "Snake, you are in big trouble. You have broken two of my laws. The first law you broke was to not eat the Human Beings. But the second law was even more important. That was to always speak the truth. There must be a consequence for those actions. From now on, you will not have those nice strong legs to walk through the forest, but must crawl across our Mother Earth on your belly.

Then Great Spirit looked at mosquito. "But you, mosquito," he said, "You have been very brave. You are the smallest of animals, and yet you stood up to snake, and you sacrificed something to save the Humans. You gave up your tongue, your speech, so that they could live. You have given, so now the Humans need to give to complete the circle. So now, whenever you hunger, the Humans will have something for you to eat: their blood. Now the circle is complete."

So, whenever a mosquito lands on you, you do not have to let him bite you. But, before you shoo him off, you might want to say "Thank you!"

STORY SIX

Raven's Story

It was Raven's responsibility to teach hunting skills to the youth of his village. The camp needed food, so Raven took his students into the forest to bring back that which was greatly needed by the people. As Raven and his group walked in the early morning hours, the dew was very heavy on the grass and rocks, so they had to remember the skills that were taught by Raven, the Teacher.

Fortunately, a deer did appear where Raven knew that deer came to feed. Raven's best student was given the first opportunity to shoot the deer skillfully enough that the deer would not suffer long. It was not meant to be, for the young student missed; and before the needed food would be lost, Raven made the sacrificial shot. The deer ran over the hill and made its last steps in the valley below. Raven and his students approached the valley and soon noticed that another person was also there.

As they approached the stranger, he looked somewhat different than they, his skin was light and he had hair on his face. There was no reason for being fearful, for they observed the way the stranger stood and how he looked at the deer. This made them feel at ease. The stranger said, "Who shot this, my relative?" And Raven said, "I did, but he did not suffer, for he is giving us his life for us to live. See, the arrow has my marking on it." The stranger looked at the deer and lifted his eyes to the group and said softly, "This is not yours, but it is mine." Raven, trying not to be disrespectful, said, "It is our way to take only what we need to survive on. We need to take it back to our people so they can eat."

The stranger seemed to want to say more, but then only said, "That is your dog, you say, standing there at your feet. Place the dog away from you and come stand by me. Now you call the dog, that you say is your dog." Having done this, Raven stood by the stranger and called the dog that he had reared since a pup, but the dog did not move. Then the stranger tenderly called for the dog to come sit at his feet, and it happened just that way. Now Raven and his young people knew that they were in the presence of a special visitor. What their eyes had seen prepared them for what their ears were going to hear, and their hearts were made ready to not forget.

The special visitor spoke in soft and yet penetrating ways. "You see, this deer is not yours. The dog that you love it not yours either. Look around. All that you see is not yours. That which covers the ground, that which grows from the ground, those animals that live upon this land and all that is above this land is given to you by your Creator for you to take care of. Never think that it is yours, but that it is a gift to be shared and respected."

247

STORY SEVEN
Legend of the Cheyennes and Pawnees

It was recently stated that a delegation of the Dog Soldier band of the Cheyennes, now living in Western Oklahoma, had visited with Skene band of Pawnees to recover two sacred arrows captured from the Cheyennes by the Pawnees more than sixty years ago. The Pawnees entertained their guests in good style and made them many presents of ponies, blankets, calico and provisions, but declined to relinquish the sacred arrows. Some years ago, while with the Chuhua Indians of Ysleta in Texas, the latter related the story of these sacred arrows, and according to the memoranda made at the time, the story is as now related. It is the Pueblo or Chihua version, but I think it will coincide with the original Cheyenne tradition. The legend runs as follows:

Many centuries ago, the Cheyennes, who were then on the great plains, were visited by a great famine. The game on which their subsistence depended had left the country and there had been none for many days. The children of the villages were gathering the bones, once used before and thrown to the dogs, and the women of the tribe managed to extract some sustenance from them by boiling them for a long time. As the children were thus engaged, there suddenly appeared among them a man wearing a long beard, who spoke the language of the Cheyennes and inquired what they were doing. Upon being informed by the children of the distress that had come upon the tribe, the stranger accompanied them to the village and told the chiefs and the people to come to a certain small cave in the vicinity the next morning, he promised to feed everyone there. No one knew the stranger nor had ever heard of his existence, though he spoke in their tongue fluently.

Early the following morning, the whole tribe appeared before the cavern, and they arranged themselves about it in a half circle. After a short time, the bearded stranger appeared at the opening of the cavern holding in each hand a piece of bark; on one piece was meat and on the other corn. He told the first Cheyenne to eat his fill, and as rapidly as the meat and corn were taken away, the pieces of bark refilled themselves, and there was no lack of food, for the pieces of bark were always full. After everyone had been fed, the bearded stranger gave the pieces of bark to the medicine man, promising they should be full of food so long as the famine lasted, and this was so.

Up to the visit of the bearded stranger, the Cheyennes had never made use of the bow and arrow, and they were unacquainted with their use. But the stranger gave the medicine man a bow and four arrows and showed the men of the Cheyennes how to make other bows and arrows and how to use them. The stranger promised that the game would return in a few days and then went on his way to the west. A few days after his departure, there was game in abundance.

For centuries, the Cheyennes carried this bow and the arrows with them in all their journeyings, which, in those days, were on foot. After many years, horses came into the country, and the Cheyennes learned to ride. In a raid made by the Cheyennes on a hostile tribe, the enemy captured the sacred bow and arrows. The Cheyennes redeemed the bow and two of the arrows by paying seven hundred horses for them. A generation or two later, while the Cheyennes were crossing a swollen stream, the sacred bow was lost, but the tribe still retained two of the arrows. The other two are still in the possession of the hostile tribe which captured them.

The Pueblos say that if a Cheyenne be accused of a serious crime before a tribunal court and be sworn upon the two sacred arrows, he will always tell the truth without regard to consequences. Every Cheyenne holds them sacred, and none has ever dared to perjure himself before them. White men from Washington have examined these arrows repeatedly, but none of them has ever been able to determine of what substance they are composed.

The foregoing is the story as told me in 1892 at Ysleta, and I regarded it as one of the many Pueblo legends, not likely to be confirmed. My surprise can, therefore, be imagined to find the legend confirmed by this telegram from Pawnee, Oklahoma, stating that even after sixty years, the Cheyenne are still endeavoring to recover the two captured arrows which they failed to redeem in their first effort. The interpretation of the bearded stranger by Chihua Pueblo Indians is that Montezuma, in one of his wanderings, encountered the Cheyennes at a time when they were in dire distress and that he assisted them in their need, as he had aided other tribes. F.E. Rousler in the OGALALLA LIGHT, reprinted in the INDIAN'S FRIEND, May, 1910.

STORY EIGHT

The Coming of the Salmon People

Two Indian hunters came rushing into camp, excited to speak with the Elder. "We have seen the sign," they said, "that a special baby has been born somewhere." The Elder said "Yes, we have seen it too! This child will be very important to all humankind, it's time for the feast to celebrate."

All the villages around were notified, and the feast was planned. At the edge of the village lived a very old woman and her Grandson. They were easily forgotten by the village; people didn't want to have them around much because they, well, they smelled awful, and their clothes were so torn.

No one let them know of the feast. Just before the feast was to begin, a little girl remembered them and went to their cabin to tell them of the celebration. The young boy wanted so much to go, but his grandmother said, "I'm sorry, but you can't go - we have nothing to give!" After pleading with his grandmother to go, she finally said, "OK, you can go!" She turned around with her back to her son, and she cried a tear drop onto a piece of leather, tied it up and gave it to the boy. "Give this to the oldest Elder and say it is for all the people!"

The joyous boy and girl went to the feast. But when the boy

walked into the feast, the people "moved away from him," some said, "Why were you invited?"

The boy straight forth walked through the gathering of people towards the oldest Elder. He placed the pouch of leather in the Elders hands and whispered to him. The Elder stood up and announced for all to hear. "This young man has brought a gift from his grandmother. He says it is a gift for all the people."

At that time the boy's grandmother walked into the feast, getting the same reaction as the boy. She stood there as the oldest Elder began opening the leather bag. A change began to come over her - the old clothes she wore became a white leather dress. Her appearance changed into a beautiful young maiden. So also changed the appearance of the boy. He became a handsomely dressed young man.

Having opened the gift, the oldest Elder held it up for all to see. It was a Salmon! Grandmother, now young girl, said, "We are Salmon People, we have been waiting to help you. Our relatives are ready to give themselves to you so you will always have food to last."

This is a YACAMA story of the coming of the Salmon People. What was the sign that caused this to occur? The Elders have been waiting and watching a certain space in the sky - a place where a special star would shine that would indicate a special baby was born, somewhere!

STORY NINE

The Story of Foolish Rabbit

How did Foolish Rabbit get his name? What lessons are to be remembered? Here is the story of the time Foolish Rabbit tried to kill Father Sun.

The Creator gave Foolish Rabbit a warm coat of fur and very big feet to enjoy the winter snows. However, when summer came, Foolish Rabbit began to wish that he didn't have the gift of furry coat. By the time Grandfather Sun stood high in the sky, Foolish Rabbit became more and more upset, even angry, at the Creator.

One day, as he was stomping around, thinking angry thoughts, a horned toad spoke saying, "Relative, why are you so angry that you do not see the shady side of the cactus there?" Foolish Rabbit went to the shady side of the cactus and rested in the coolness. After sleeping awhile, he woke up even hotter than before. The sun had moved on toward its home in the west. Foolish Rabbit became even more upset with not only the Creator but now the great Sun as well.

Now, Foolish Rabbit knew exactly where Grandfather Sun left his home in the eastern sky to begin his daily journey. A plan began to form in his mind. Being exceptionally good with the bow and arrow, as only Foolish Rabbit could brag, he decided to go shoot·

the sun before it could rise up to heat the day.

When night came and Grandfather Sun had entered the back door to his lodge in the west, Foolish Rabbit started his journey. He ran all night to the eastern doorway of Grandfather Sun. Getting there just before sunrise, he hid behind a large rock. When Grandfather Sun stood in the doorway ready to start across the sky, Foolish Rabbit darted out from his hiding place and shot an arrow straight into Grandfather Sun's side. Then he turned around and ran as fast as he could. He wasn't sure what would happen next.

As Foolish Rabbit retreated from the wounded Sun, he began to feel very hot. He looked over his shoulder and saw a terrible thing - hot molten lava was flowing from Grandfather Sun's side right toward him. The lava was burning everything in sight, changing the beauty of trees, flowers and land into ashes of darkness. Foolish Rabbit became very frightened and yelled out to anyone to help him. Suddenly, a yellow bush called to him, "You Foolish Rabbit! Haven't you ever thought about going under ground?" "Oh!" said Foolish Rabbit, "I didn't think of that." Yellow bush continued, "Dig here at my roots, hold onto them until what you have done passes over."

The yellow bush began to prepare itself for this unexpected purification. Foolish Rabbit felt this in the roots of the bush as he held on tightly with all four feet. Above, many sounds were heard - animals running, birds calling to each other, the wind blowing. Then came the fiery lava which had no mercy for any living thing. The lava covered the yellow bush. Foolish Rabbit felt all of this through the roots of his friend the bush. He tried to comfort yellow bush. He told him how sorry he was and that he would never do such a foolish thing again. He asked the bush to forgive him. Not one sound was heard from yellow bush.

Yellow bush was quiet for a long, long time. Foolish Rabbit became anxious to go above ground, so he released his tight grip and started to climb upward. It was then the Yellow Bush spoke, but ever so weakly, "It is too soon to go up." But, Foolish Rabbit continued on. Reaching the top, he looked at the destruction that he had caused. Every beauty was changed to colorless ash. Spellbound, he lingered too long and some sparks of fire hit his coat of fur. He quickly retreated underground once again to the comfort of Yellow Bush's roots. His impatience left him with scorched spots on his coat and a very damaged spirit.

Some time later, Yellow Bush said, "If you want, you can return to the above world and see what has happened there." Foolish Rabbit was glad to hear a little stronger voice from his dear friend. Before going up, he said, "Thank you my dear friend. I will always remember what you have done for me."

On top, Foolish Rabbit walked in a daze. How could the actions of one small creature do so much damage, change so much beauty? He thought that the world could never go back to the beauty it was before. For weeks Rabbit was stunned and depressed. Then, as he was sitting there, a little voice came out near the surface. A little green plant stuck its head out and said, "Hello there! I'm coming back! But Foolish Rabbit knew that it would take many years for it to fully return. He promised to never be angry with the Creator again and to always honor Grandfather Sun.

Now, as for Grandfather Sun, he also vowed to never again come up in the same doorway, but to always move over a distance before coming up each day - just in case some other Foolish Rabbit wanted to shoot him!

To this very day, that yellow bush has accepted a part of his foolish friend's name. It is called the Rabbit Bush.

STORY TEN

The Wolf's Vision Quest

You see, all the animals are teachers. The wolf is especially called "the trailblazer" because he makes new trails for us to follow.

Once there was a village and all the people there were wolf people. The chief had a dream that the Creator came to him and told him that he had to go on a Vision Quest. He had to go into the outer forest and learn about himself. Then he was to come back and share with the wolf village what he had learned.

So Wolf decided to make his preparations. He went to his friends and told them what he must do. They all wished him a good journey.

Now Wolf went out to the outer forest and really began to have a good time chasing animals, enjoying the warm Sun and all the creation in the forest. Soon he began to get sleepy, so he laid down thinking, "I'll just take a little nap now." The place where Wolf chose to make his bed was under a shade tree where the grass was green and was nice and soft.

Then, all of a sudden, something woke him up; he realized

257

that he was really hungry. Wolf saw a rabbit, and he began to chase it. The rabbit darted this way and that, back and forth, trying to trick the wolf. Wolf chased the rabbit into some real thick bushes. The rabbit kept going into smaller and smaller places. The bush was really thick and had sharp, long thorns on it. You see, the wolf, being bigger than the rabbit, got himself into a real fix as he went further into the bush. Finally, the wolf got so stuck in that bush he couldn't get out!

All of the sharp thorns began to pierce his skin all over. As he tried to move, it only caused more pain. Then the bugs who lived in the bush began to bite him in the places that the thorns had already pierced. Wolf began to get scared now and tried to get away. He soon realized he was completely stuck and hurting all over his body.

Wolf began to feel very sad. No one was there to help him and soon he began to cry. He couldn't figure out a way out of this predicament. He was stuck, couldn't move, and getting bitten all over, and so he just sat there and cried himself to sleep.

In his sleep, wolf had a vision. His spirit helpers came to him and said, "If you use your gift of patience and your gift of thinking and use the medicine that is carried on your tongue, then you can get yourself out of this mess."

With that, Wolf woke up. He thought about his vision. "I must use my gift of patience, being in my own sacred space, being in the center of myself where I am not yelling or crying." He began to think more and more about his vision.

While he was thinking, he remembered a part of his vision that was about using the medicine he carried on his tongue. His spirit helper had said that he could get himself out of this mess. "How do I do this?" he kept asking himself.

Wolf decided that by using his tongue, he could get the thorns out of his skin and fur. Then he could lick all those hurt places. So Wolf carefully took out each thorn and piled them up in a small heap one at a time. Where he was wounded, he used the medicine that was on his tongue and licked his wounds. So Wolf did this; he took care of all his wounds.

Then Wolf began to think about all the insects that were biting him. He remembered that he had just crashed into their house, their sacred space without any permission. He realized why they had gotten upset. They were probably thinking, "Who is this guy anyway, just coming in here and messing up our sacred space!" Of course they were upset! So, Wolf apologized to them. He remembered that their space was sacred to them too.

Thinking a lot more clearly now and having much more patience, he thought, "If I am really honest with my heart, there must surely be a path out of here." It is said that Grandmother Spider opened a path for Wolf. She took some of the bush out of the way so

259

that Wolf could see how to get out of his trap. So, with Wolf's gift of patience and thinking, the medicine on his tongue and his apologies, Wolf got himself out of the mess he was in.

It took Wolf a couple of days to get back to his village. As he returned, he reminded himself that he must share with his people what lessons he had learned on his Vision Quest. So Wolf did. Everyone was so excited to see their Wolf Chief. They had missed him, and they wanted to know what he had experienced in the Outer Forest. Wolf shared all with them in the Council Ring. He shared his stories and his lessons.

Afterwards, they had a big feast which we call the Thanksgiving Feast. During this time we share about life, and we always say thank you to the Creator for all of life's lessons.

260

STORY ELEVEN

Clay Pot Boy

Born to a Pueblo couple was a baby girl. She was to be their only child. As she grew up and learned the family trade of pottery making, she was very kind to her parents but showed no interest in boys. Even as a young beautiful lady she would not even so to where there were boys. She also would not go to gather water with the other girls.

Her mother was becoming very concerned that her daughter would never bring them a grandson or granddaughter. She went to gather clay thinking to herself about her daughter. The Spirit of the spring heard her thoughts. She often would get upset with her daughter and speak of wanting grandchildren, but her daughter would continue being kind and loving with her mother.

One day while the young girl was gathering clay near the river, the Spirit of the River placed "the seed of life" into the clay she gathered. She took the clay home, and while she was molding clay bowls, the seed of life entered the young girl. In the months that followed, the girl's mother became even more upset with the coming of a baby without a father. Also, she was angry with her daughter saying; "What will people say?" Now the girl's father was very happy with the coming baby child. He couldn't wait to share his stories and the hunting with the child, regardless of the situation.

261

When the baby was delivered, another thing was discovered, he had no arm or legs but he had a mouth at the top of his head. "The young girl's baby was a clay pot baby!" Grandfather was so happy that he named him, Clay Pot Boy. Grandmother could not accept him for a long time, still wanting "a real baby."

Clay Pot Boy grew very rapidly, and in just twenty days, he was running (rather rolling) around with the other children. The other boys accepted Clay Pot Boy because he was such a pleasant boy to be around, and Clay Pot Boy had such a good mouth to catch balls with! Clay Pot Boy longed to have evenings come so that he could listen to his grandfather tell stories and learn their heritage.

After the first snow of the winter, Clay Pot Boy rushed home to speak with his grandfather. "Grandfather, you said we are to hunt for rabbits after the first snow came!" Now grandfather was trying to be understanding said, "Well, grandson, you are right, but how can this work out?" Clay Pot Boy thought for awhile then he said, "We can hunt together, you hide and I'll chase the rabbit back to you."

The very next morning they left early to hunt all day together in the light snow. By about mid-morning they had gotten ten rabbits, so grandfather sat down and rested. Clay Pot Boy went off to enjoy rolling around. He rolled up this hill and down, picked an especially tall hill to roll down, but halfway down Clay Pot Boy began rolling so fast that he couldn't control himself and smashed into a large rock.

262

Grandfather, having waited so long, began to look for Clay Pot Boy and called to him, but no answer came. After hours of waiting he sat down on a rock and was very sad, for he had surely lost his grandson.

From the broken pieces of clay a miracle happened. A real human boy arose out of the pieces of clay. A handsome, strong boy with such a bright spirit came into being. So Clay Pot Boy (now boy) saw his grandfather depressed and saddened over the love of his grandson. Clay Pot Boy had a trick thought, so he went over and said, " What is wrong? Why are you so sad?" His grandfather told him, "I have lost my grandson; we loved him so!" Grandfather then ask, "Have you seen Clay Pot Boy?" Still teasing the boy answered, "No! I didn't see anyone." Then Clay Pot Boy said, "Grandfather, it's me! I have became a boy!" For awhile grandfather did not understand, but he became convinced when Clay Pot Boy told him of the many things they had shared with each other.

Returning home with the rabbits, Clay Pot Boy and grandfather told grandmother and his mother what had happened. Grandmother was over joyed to finally have a real grandson.

Years later, Clay Pot Boy began to want to know about his father. His mother had told him of her nearness to the water where she gathers clay. So Clay Pot Boy often went there. This time a voice spoke, "Clay Pot Boy, you have a father! He waits for you in the Underworld." The Spirit of the Water told the boy to walk into the spring water, and he would see his father.

Clay Pot Boy did this, traveling into the most beautiful place he had ever seen. The people were so loving and joyous, and everything was so green and colorful. Then he met his father. His father told Clay Pot Boy of his love for his mother but knew she would not return that love. Now he wanted Clay Pot Boy to return to the above the ground world and tell his mother that he waits for her. He wants the family to be together here in the beautiful under-the-surface world.

Clay Pot Boy felt and knew his father's love and, returned through the water to tell his mother of the news.

When he got back home, his mother was very sick. They tried every medicine they knew to cure her, every healing song, every prayer. But Clay Pot Boy's mother died. Clay Pot Boy said, "I will go back to live with my father below the water." He walked back to the spring and found his father waiting there beside the water. Together they traveled down to the land below. When they arrived, Clay Pot Boy was very surprised to find his mother waiting for him. His father explained that the land below was a Spirit Land.

So now a truly happy life came to them. If you were to sit by that spring, you would hear the laughter of that happy family . . . Clay Pot Boy and his mother and father in that land below the water.

STORY TWELVE

Must Gather to Continue Life

A story is told of a man known to the tribe as a prophet, a visionary. He had told the people that he had received a vision of the snow to be so deep this coming winter it would reach the top of the trees. This coming winter would be the end of the world, and the people need to get prepared for this.

The prophet in his sleep one night was carried by a spirit to take him through the four layers above to the council in the sky by a messenger. The Council told him that they had looked into the sacred box, and it is only half full. An extension of life had been granted for hundreds of years if the people would get rid of all barriers that separate them, always speak with love and affection for each other, and care for the children as they were the pillars of the tribe. Tell them they must all love everyone as if they were a family.

The Council further instructed the prophet to "tell the people to build a big lodge enough for all to gather in the spring and the fall to share the Sacred Pipe and dance the dance of Life." They were to hold harmony within themselves and with each other. "Then you will be blessed by the spirits."

When the prophet awoke he told the people of his vision, the reasons for life to continue and the ceremonies to take place each

265

year to celebrate life. To this day they still remember the time when life was almost at an end. Ever since, the Chippewas have held the Ogemah Dance in the spring and the fall, as a reminder of the vision and of the spirits desire that they live in peace with each other and with all people.

STORY THIRTEEN

The Path Without End

New Leaf (Eshkebug) lived with his parents far from any humankind. He was content with the trees, flowers, birds and animals that provided him with great companionship. With early spring, New Leaf had become restless, so he wandered further and further from his home during his hunting.

One day New Leaf came upon a strange path. It was a clearly defined circular track, and the growth had been worn away by tiny prints of small, delicate, moccasined feet. Here was a path without end.

The center of the circle had been pushed down heavily. No animal he knew of could have made such a print in the grass. Then New Leaf heard music pulsating, swelling and diminishing, coming closer and closer. From the west, high in the sky, came a star flash. Slowly a sky-craft moved downward, feather-like. New Leaf hid himself in the bushes to watch as the ship, like a giant clam, landed in the circular path.

The music stopped, and from the opening at the top of the ship came joyous laughter. Ten beautiful maidens stepped out onto the path around the sky-craft. They played with a glowing ball, then danced with the grace and lightness of young deer. Sitting in the grass, keeping very near their sky-craft, they gathered flowers and wove them into garlands for one another. They rose and stepped back into their ship. As the top closed, the maidens sang the melody which moved their sky-craft, and it vanished into the sky.

New Leaf raced home and told his parents of what he had seen. His mother remembered old stories told by her family of such as this, but she said nothing.

New Leaf returned to the clearing the very next day. He again witnessed the landing of the ship and the dancing of the maidens. It was the youngest of the maidens who caused New Leaf's heart to rise to his throat. He stood up and called out while stepping out into the open, holding his hands before him to show that he meant no harm. The young maiden screamed and they all jumped back into their ship, sang their flight song, and left New Leaf standing there alone.

Seeing her son's sadness, his mother then spoke at length of the sky people and their special powers which are not possessed by the Earthbound. She said that a sky woman would never be content on Earth.

New Leaf was determined to keep his love for the maiden he longed to marry. His mother said that the sky people were unaware of time as it existed for mortals, as they were immortal. If he was to marry one, he himself would grow old and die, and she would still be very young.

Day after day, New Leaf visited the grove, but no sky-craft descended. Night time came and he slept. As he slept, he dreamed of a handsome young buck who approached New Leaf without fear. Suddenly, the stag changed into a man dressed in deerskins. In his hand he carried a belt fashioned of braided hides. Around him shone a radiance of blue light.

"Your heart is known to me, New Leaf," he said. "Since you have been sincere in your concern for the deer people, never neglecting to beg our pardon when you took our lives in your need, we feel kindly disposed to you. Therefore, we, the deer people, confer upon you the ability to change your shape as you will. Such a power is yours only as you find it necessary in your quest of the moon maiden. Yes, New Leaf, it is from Grandmother Moon that the craft first came. Use this power wisely, and know that the deer people favor you. We will help you as we are able. Here is the symbol of your medicine." He then pressed the belt into New Leaf's hand. When New Leaf awoke, the belt was tied firmly around his waist.

For many days, New Lead waited. Then, on a sunny afternoon, the sky people came. Before the craft landed, he ran to the edge of the path without end, touched his belt and willed himself to become a tree. The sky-craft landed, but took off again after seeing a tree was not there before.

New Leaf watched the craft leave again, returned to his

269

former shape, saddened again. He was not going to give up, so he decided to fast and pray. In his sleep the stag came to him again out of the woods. "When they come again you become a fawn, and I will be the doe near you. What maiden can resist the appealing sight of a young one and helpless one?" With a smile the stag vanished.

The sky-craft did finally appear in the sky, and New Leaf was ready. As the youngest maiden came near and knelt to stroke the fawn's velvet muzzle, New Leaf willed himself a man and seized her. Her traveling companions were shocked, ran to their sky-craft and sang their flying song.

All afternoon the craft lingered as the maidens waited, hoping their sister would somehow escape from the fearful creature that had captured her. Finally at twilight the craft left; no more would they return.

With the sky maiden, New Leaf returned to his home. Many times New Leaf tried to assure his captured maiden that he was not to be feared. The maiden was not to be comforted by New Leaf, and then his mother knew what to do. She enfolded the frightened girl in her arms and rocked her as a little girl. Soon she stopped shivering, accepted food and went to sleep.

They named her Sky Woman, and she was treated with much love and kindness. Sky Woman began to accept her new situation, she helped with the chores and eventually became New Leaf's wife.

A son was born to a now happy couple, and they named him Blue Sky. New Leaf was extremely happy. Yet over time New Leaf would often see a great sadness in his wife's eyes. New Leaf was the gentlest and best of husbands. However, Sky Woman was glad that he had chosen her to capture; now she was content to be his wife.

One night she was discovered quietly sobbing New Leaf held her tenderly as she told him her dream. She saw her parents, now grown old, heard them call her to their side. They had asked to see their grandson before they died. Each knew that this could not be.

Blue Sky grew, and so did his mother's longing to visit her parents. Now New Leaf wanted to comfort his wife, so he built a replica of the sky-ship out of birch bark. Sky Woman was so happy to be able to sit in it with her sewing. Blue Sky and his mother would often sit, and she would tell him stories of her people.

One afternoon as they were within the birch bark ship, Blue Sky said, "Mother, please sing the flight song for me!" His mother laughed, "It's a Women's song, son. Still, I will sing it for you, only if you promise never to repeat a note . . ." "I promise, mother," said Blue Sky.

Sky Woman began to sing, lost in the memories, unaware that the ship lifted, floated above the trees and in the sky, quickly landing before the lodge of Sky Woman's parents. This reunion brought much laughter and feasting. But on earth there was great sorrow.

271

New Leaf believed that he had made her happy, and she loved him so. He could not understand why she would leave and take their lovely son. Once again seeking guidance, New Leaf fasted prayed and meditated until the stag deer stepped from the woods. He turned into a man surrounded by Blue Light. He spoke briefly, "Only wait, New Leaf, wait. Perhaps you will wait forever. Wait. Hope. Do not give up." Then he was gone.

Blue Sky missed his father so much that he begged his mother, "Let us go home, mother." "Soon" she replied. But time for the sky people had little meaning. So Blue Sky finally asked his grandparents, "Could you send for my father?" Because they loved their grandchild, they agreed. "Go," they said, "Bring your father back, tell him we expect a gift of a bird of every kind. Take your mother's eldest sister as pilot for your craft, for she is wise and will help you."

In the valley of his birth, Blue Sky found his father, old now and very lonely. Blue Sky told his father of how they flew to his mother's parents, that Sky Woman had not deserted him with intention, but by accident.

With a captured bird of every kind, they traveled to the moon. New Leaf gave his father-in-law the birds he had asked for. The birds were released, flying straight into the skies, becoming a new group of stars.

STORY FOURTEEN

The Sacred Spring and Gifts of Corn and Meat

Among the Native people a drought had stopped the crops from growing. The people asked the medicine people to fast and go into the hills and seek a dream, see what the Great Creator would have them to do. So the Cheyenne people gathered around to sit together to talk about the drought and the famine. While the village people talked, there appeared a medicine man named "Tall Pine." He was dressed in a beautiful buffalo robe, and his face was painted with dream designs. His feathers were arranged carefully in a certain way. The people were surprised to see the medicine man fully dressed.

Suddenly a second medicine man appeared, and he too was dressed in a beautiful buffalo robe, face painted with dream designs just like Tall Pine, and feathers arranged also in the same way. The people were really surprised to see both medicine men dressed exactly alike.

It seemed strange! Tall Pine asked, "My friend, what do you have against me that you dressed the same way I do?" The second medicine man replied, "I'm Big Tree. And, my friend, you do me an injustice. It was my dream that told us to dress this way." Tall Pine replied, "In my dream I was told to dress this way and told to go to a certain spring were I was to meet someone."

273

Since both medicine men had similar dreams, they decided to both go to the sacred spring and see who was right!

All the people followed as they finally arrived at the sacred spring. Then both Tall Pine and Big Tree stepped into the spring and immediately sank to the bottom, completely dropping from sight.

When they got to the bottom of the spring, they saw a beautiful and most wonderful woman. "Why have you come?" said the woman. Then answered the medicine man, "We have come because we both had the same dream. You told us how to paint our faces, dress and arrange our feathers. Our people are hungry; we both want to help our people."

"My friends," said the woman, "you are both right. Your hearts are the same and so I appeared to you in a vision. Here is a bowl of food for each one of you. Take it back to your people, and you shall never be hungry again." In one bowl was corn, in the other was pounded meat called pemmican.

The two men took the bowls and ran to the surface of the spring. The people were happy to see that the two medicine men had followed their dream and had brought back with them food. All of the tribe ate from the two bowls of food, and no matter how much they ate, the bowls were always full of food.

Then the people were very thankful to the woman under the

surface of the Sacred Spring for her generous deed and how she saved the tribe from hunger.

The medicine man later had a dream of the same woman. And she said, "My name is Earth Woman. I will always take care of my Earth Children who have faith, and they will never go hungry." That is why the earth is full of gifts and plants for us to eat. People will never go hungry again.

This is a legend told by the Cheyenne of how their people first came to have the corn and pounded meat that give them strength.

STORY FIFTEEN

The Last Rose

Roses were one the most numerous and brilliantly colored of all the flowers. Such were their numbers and such were the variety and richness of their shades, they were common. No one paid much attention to them; their beauty went un-noticed, their glory unsung.

Even when their numbers declined and their colors faded, no one appeared to care. Cycles of scarcity and plenty had occurred. There was no cause for alarm. There is degeneration and regeneration. Plenty always follows scarcity.

But year after year, roses became fewer in number. All the numbers and richness of the flowers diminished, the fatness of the rabbits increased. Only the bear, the bee, and the hummingbird were aware that something was wrong.

The Anishinabe felt that something was not quite right, but they couldn't explain it. They only knew that the bear was thinner and that the bear's flesh was less sweet than formerly. The bears found smaller quantities of honey, and what they found was less delectable. The bees and hummingbirds found fewer roses. The Anishinabe were bewildered; the bears blamed the bees; the bees were alarmed. But no one could do anything.

276

Eventually, one summer there were no roses. Bees hungered; hummingbirds grew thin; the bear raged. In later years, that summer was known as the Summer of the Disappearance of the Rose. At last, everyone was alarmed. In desperation, a great meeting was called. Everyone was invited.

There were many days of discussion before the meeting decided to dispatch all the swift to search the world for a single rose, and, if they found one, to bring it back. Months went by before a hummingbird chanced to discover a solitary rose growing and clinging to a mountainside in a far-off land.

The hummingbird lifted the plant and pulled the rose from its bed and brought it back. On arrival, medicine men and women immediately tended the rose and in a few days restored the rose to life. When he was well enough, the rose was able to give an account of the destruction of the roses.

In a voice quivering with weakness, the rose said, "The rabbits ate all the roses."

The assembly raised an angry uproar. At the word, the bears and wolves and lynxes seized the rabbits by the ears and cuffed them. During the assault the rabbits' ears were stretched and their mouths were split open. The outraged animals might have killed all the rabbits that day had not the rose interceded on their behalf saying, "Had you cared and watched us, we might have survived. But you

277

were unconcerned. Our destruction was partly your fault. Leave the rabbits be."

Reluctantly the angry animals released the rabbits. While the rabbits wounds eventually healed, they did not lose their scars which remained as marks of their intemperance. Nor did the roses ever attain their former brilliance or abundance. Instead the roses received from Nanabush thorns to protect them from the avarice of the hungry and the intemperate.

Nanabush, in endowing the roses with thorns, warned the assembly, "You can take the life of plants, but you cannot give them life."*

*From, *Ojibway Heritage*, Basil Johnston

STORY SIXTEEN

The Pipe and the Eagle

The Anishinabe people now had received the Clan System and the Midewiwin ceremonies. A long period of peace and prosperity was experienced by all; cultural ways blossomed.

However, in time, conflict and warfare began to appear again on the Earth. Conflict became so prevalent that almost all of the people's time was consumed in the preparations for war and in the making of war. Even the ceremonies became oriented to conflict so that a tribe or band might gain spiritual guidance or favor that they could use to gain more territory. More and more of the religious teachings were twisted to apply to conflict instead of the life-giving ways of the Midewiwin. Fractions began to emerge within the tribes out of which warrior societies developed. Elitism became the example for young people to follow instead of peace, humility and generosity. Face painting grew as a practice among the people as pride overcame humility. Soon there were too few hunters left to provide for the families. The hunters became the proud and vain warriors.

At this time, the spirit of Wahnaboozhoo emerged among the people. He had the Sacred Pipe wrapped in sage. Wahnaboozhoo showed the people how to smoke tobacco in the pipe and, in so doing, seal peace, brotherhood and sisterhood among the bands, tribes and nations. He told the people that the smoke that came from the pipe would carry their thoughts and prayers to the Creator just as their tobacco offerings in the fire would do.

Wahnaboozhoo told the people how to make the pipe out of the sacred pipestone in the Earth and how to carve the pipestem from sumac.

With the coming of the pipe, honor returned to be a guiding principle for life for many people. The sacredness of a person's word became, once again, foremost in day-to-day transactions.

The conflict and warfare subsided.

Still, the seed was planted to use the Midewiwin and its spirited powers for selfish concerns.

After some time, there came to be people who chose to use the Midewiwin as a way to build up their own personal power. They sought to instill <u>fear</u> in other people by harnessing spiritual powers and using them in negative ways. There were those that even took the lives of others and distorted the lives of their rivals by using their spiritual medicine in a bad way.

This was clearly against the intentions of the Creator, who was greatly concerned at how such a beautiful gift could be so twisted and corrupted. The Creator then instructed a very powerful being to destroy the Earth after the sun rose four times. It looked as though all life on the Earth would be destroyed again.

Just before dawn on the fourth day, the eagle flew out of the crack between night and day. He flew straight into the Sky. He flew so high that he flew completely out of sight. He flew to talk with the Creator. The Sun was about to come over the rim of the Earth. The eagle screamed four times to get the Creator's attention. The Creator saw the eagle and held back the Sun. At the time of this "false dawn," the eagle talked to the Creator. He said, "I know the Earth is full of corruption and is out of balance. I have seen all this. But also I have seen that there are yet a few people who have remained true to their instructions. I still see the smoke of tobacco rise here and there from humble people who are still trying to live in harmony with the Universe. I plead on behalf of these few that you call off the destruction of the Earth. Let me fly over the Earth each day at dawn and look over the people. As long as I can report to you each day that there is still one person who sounds the Waterdrum or who uses tobacco and the Pipe in the proper way, I beg you to spare the Earth for the sake of the unborn. It is in these unborn that there is still hope for the Earth's people to correct their ways."

The Creator pondered what the eagle had to say, then instructed the spiritual being to hold back the destruction of the Earth. The Creator entrusted the eagle with the duty of reporting each day the conditions of the Earth people. The miracle of the sunrise happened again for the Anishinabe.

We owe our lives and the lives of our children to the eagle. This is why the eagle is so respected by Native and natural people everywhere. This is why Indian people make a whistle from the wingbone of the eagle. They sound this whistle four times at the start of their ceremonies. They do this to call in the powers of the spirits. They do this to remember our brother, the eagle and the role he plays in the preservation of the Earth.*

*From *The Mishomis Book* by Edward Benton-Banai.

INDEX

283

285

286

Suggested Readings

Andrews, Ted. Animal Speak: *The Spiritual and Magical Powers of Creatures Great and Small*. Minnesota: Llewellyn Publications, 1993.

Argüells, José. *The Mayan Factor: Path Beyond Technology*. New Mexico: Bear & Company, 1987.

Benton-Banai, Edward. *The Mishomis Book: The Voice of the Ojibway*. Minnesota: Indian Country Press & Publications, Inc., 1979.

Boatman, John. *My Elders Taught Me: Aspects of Western Great Lakes American Indian Philosophy*. Maryland: University Press of America, Inc., 1992.

Brown, Joseph Epes. *The Sacred Pipe: Black Elk's Account of the Seven Rites of the Oglala Sioux*. Recorded and edited by Joseph Epes Brown. Norman, OK: University of Oklahoma Press, 1953.

Eagle Man, Ed McGaa. *Mother Earth Spirituality*. New York: Harper Collins Publishers, 1990.

Four Worlds Development Project. *The Sacred Tree*. WI: Lotus Light, 1989.

Freesoul, John Redtail. *Breath of the Invisible - The Way of the Pipe*. Ill: The Theosophical Publishing House, 1986.

Freidel, David, Linda Schele and Joy Parker. *Maya Cosmos: Three Thousand Years on the Shaman's Path.* New York: First Quill Edition, 1993.

Grey Owl and Little Pigeon. *Cry of the Ancients.* Missouri: Herald Publishing House, 1974.

Hanson, L. Taylor. *He Walked The Americas.* Wisconsin. Amherst Press, 1963.

Johnston, Basil. *Ojibway Heritage.* Lincoln: University of Nebraska Press, 1976.

Mails, Thomas. *Fools Crow.* Lincoln: University of Nebraska Press, 1979.

McFadden, Steven. *Profiles In Wisdom: Native Elders Speak About the Earth.* Santa Fe, NM: Bear & Company Publishing, 1991.

Medicine Eagle, Brooke. *Buffalo Woman Comes Singing: The Spirit Song Of A Rainbow Medicine Woman.* New York: Ballatine Books, 1991.

Neihardt, John G. *Black Elk Speaks.* New York: William Morrow and Company, 1932.

Nitsch, Twylah and Jamie Sams. *Other Council Fires Were Here Before Ours.* New York: Harper Collins Publishers, 1991.

Peterson, Scott. *Native American Prophecies.* New York: Paragon House, 1990.

Powers, William K. *Oglala Religion*. University of Nebraska Press, 1977.

Ross, Allen Charles. *Mitakuye Oyasin*. Ft. Yates, ND: Bear, 1989.

Storm, Hyemeyohsts. *Seven Arrows*. New York: Ballantine Books, 1972.

Willoya, William and Vinson Brown. *Warriors of the Rainbow*. Healdsburg, CA: Naturegraph Publishers, Inc., 1962.

MAIL ORDER FORM
FOR THE BOOK ENTITLED:
THE UNIVERSAL PEACE SHIELD OF TRUTHS:
ANCIENT AMERICAN INDIAN PEACE SHIELD TEACHINGS

		TOTAL
1-5 COPIES	$14.95 EA	
6 - 12 COPIES	$13.95 EA	
13 OR MORE COPIES	$12.95 EA	
POSTAGE (BOOK RATE)		
1-10 COPIES Add $1.90 per book		
11 OR MORE COPIES $14.00		
HANDLING CHARGE - ADD $1.50 PER ORDER		
	TOTAL	

Make checks or money orders payable to: (No Credit Card Orders)

Rolland J. Williston
Box 1434
Angel Fire, NM 87710

Your Address:
Name_____
Address_____
City, State, Zip_____

Wholesale orders welcome - **contact Rolland J. Williston**